THE FINANCIAL
ADVISOR
TO BUILDING
WEALTH

*PURSUING PROSPERITY
WITH FINANCIAL EDUCATION*

Thomas Herold - Spring 2011 Edition

The Financial Advisor to Building Wealth

Pursuing Prosperity
with Financial Education

Spring 2011 Edition

Revision 1.1

Thomas Herold
Dream Manifesto, LLC.
© 2005-2011 All rights reserved.

www.wealthbuildingcourse.com

Table of Contents

INTRODUCTION

"Pursuing Prosperity with Financial Education"

Introduction

Welcome to the Financial Advisor to Building Your Wealth

It's my pleasure to present the Spring 2011 edition of our quarterly publication 'Financial Advisor to Building Wealth'.

Just take a moment and think about what wealth means to you. If you're like most folk, you think it's all about money. It was for me too, until I decided to explore the topic more deeply and really consider what makes us wealthy, prosperous people. Wealth, for me, is not merely material possessions: it's your health, your lifestyle and relationships, even your mental abilities.

Curious yet? If you still think money has anything to do with wealth, you'll be in for a big surprise when you read this issue. My main aim, and the inspiration for my website and the whole of my work, is to help you learn about finance like I did – to help you transform your life, leave the past behind and take control of your wealth. Now, you might think financial terminology is about as interesting as a bag of rice falling off a shelf in China. But these days, one of the most essential and precious gifts you can give yourself is a financial education - especially given the worldwide economic crisis we are all experiencing.

Humanity is embarking on the biggest transfer of wealth in history. You may have sensed it already, and you're right: wealth is flowing at breathtaking speeds away from the financially uneducated towards people who know about finance and, crucially, how to use that knowledge to their advantage.

The current international financial crisis is a direct outcome of government and bank interventions. It's time for us to open our eyes to this and start to protect ourselves.

You might have heard the phrase, "If you always do what you've always done, you'll always get what you've always got." There's no question that, in order to secure your future and live a life that you're in control of, you must take on the task of understanding what is happening to your hard-earned money.

Once you grasp and unravel the hidden agenda of a few powerful people, you will be able to choose and reclaim your financial freedom. At the moment, this may all sound like a conspiracy theory to you; however, the research and facts contained in this book will provide you with enough evidence that there is a plan behind all this, which right now is serving other people, not you.

You'll realize that this plan is nothing new, and that the past shows similar attempts at monetary control and failure. Learning about these will make you better able to react to the present, and start creating wealth for yourself, rather than other people.

I've structured the articles into several categories. Feel free to skip between them and simply read what interests you most. Remember: this is not a course that you're doing for anyone else. This is a gift to yourself. Read the articles that apply to you, and in doing so you will broaden your knowledge and feel more qualified to keep learning and growing your wealth.

All the articles have been taken from the Wealth Building Course website and assembled here for you to make your financial learning simpler and more convenient. I've left out several articles which focused on issues that have now been overtaken by events. The situation is constantly changing, but the articles here have been carefully selected for their continuing relevance.

Enjoy your reading and always keep learning. Allow your mind to open up to new ideas. Believe that you can change your approach to wealth, and transform your life. As Steve Jobs once said: "Stay hungry, stay foolish."

Thomas Herold

Introduction

<u>INVESTING</u>

"Putting Energy to Work"

Investing

How to Save and Invest 10 Percent of Your Income in 2011

It is that time of the year again, the time when you and everyone else start making your New Year's Resolutions.

There are many good resolutions that you can make, ranging from the goal to start going to the gym to spending more time at home with your family.

One resolution that you should not neglect as you go into the year 2011 concerns your finances. This is a good time to make a practical New Year's Resolution to both save and invest fully ten percent of all your income this next year.

Why Save 10 Percent of Your Income in 2011?

You may be wondering what is so important about first saving and then investing ten percent of your income in the New Year. Ten percent is more than simply a convenient round number to throw out at you. It is the amount that financial experts say you should be saving every month anyway. Not only this, but they suggest that you should save minimally ten percent of all your take home pay, or the money that you actually get to deposit to your bank account every pay period.

There are many reasons to save this amount of money when times are reasonably good.

First of all, you are building up a cushion of financial reserves for rainy days. Financial experts call this an emergency fund. The idea is that you should have anywhere from three months to six months worth of your costs of living kept in such a liquid and readily accessible fund.

You probably shrug your shoulders in bewilderment when you hear that you should keep as much as half a year's worth of living expenses on hand. If you were to suffer a serious illness and be unable to work for a time, or even lose your job, you would see how essential this money would become.

Why Invest 10 Percent of Your Income in 2011?

So far, you have just read about the first half of the New Year's Resolution equation, that of saving ten percent of your income in 2011. You should do more than this though. You should set aside your emergency fund money and then save ten percent of your take home pay this New Year. You must get serious about saving for retirement if you are ever going to achieve it. This is an ideal time to make the resolution to make it happen.

Now you should know that necessary retirement savings amounts for you will depend on where you are in your working career and goals. It may be that ten percent is not enough for you to catch up if you are already forty to fifty and have little money set aside.

A helpful way to take the factors of your age, hoped for retirement age, annual income, anticipated inflation, and returns on investment all into account is through using what is known as an online retirement savings calculator. It will tell you what percentage of your money that you personally need to save. Ten percent is a good place to start.

Elements That Impact the Money That You Should Save and Invest

When you make your New Year's Resolution for saving and investing money this coming year, the exact amount that you settle on is a truly personal decision. Ten percent is a good minimum goal, but individual factors that affect you and your family could cause you to adjust this amount. Your personal financial goals should impact this rate of savings and investing.

If you dream of an retiring earlier than the sixty year minimum that the IRS commonly assumes so that you can travel the globe, then you should plan to save and invest a greater amount than ten percent every month in order to achieve such goals.

Similarly, if you help to support a spouse who is not working, several children, or even an aging parent, then you may come to the conclusion that you should save and invest a greater percentage rate than ten percent in order to effectively plan for the future. Also, your job may not be as stable as you would like it to be. This argues for saving more than ten percent of your money so that you will be financially more secure if you become suddenly unemployed.

How Can You Begin To Save and Invest Money Every Month?

It is one thing to make a New Year's Resolution with the best of intentions and another thing altogether to actually keep it. This is why the overwhelming majority of such resolutions fail within only the first one to two months. In fact, seventy-eight percent of people who make these resolutions every year abandon them in failure. One of the main ways to avoid falling into this majority is to make a plan that you can stick with to see through your important goal to save and invest ten percent of your income.

You can reach most any goal in life if you plan properly in advance. This is not so difficult as you might initially think. Saving and investing your money requires a first significant step. You have to start by either creating, or if you already have one by altering, your monthly budget.

Tips to Make A Budget Yield Savings

There are several things that you can do to a budget in order to come up with extra money every month for savings. One of them is to reduce an extra expense that you do not need from the budget each month. You could cut back your daily newspaper delivery to only weekend delivery, or cut the service entirely. You might order in a pizza every week instead of going out to dinner one night. You can also stop your cable service in favor of a cheaper Netflix membership.

It is also a good idea to set up an automatic paycheck transfer. These allow for you to put a certain percentage of your paycheck straight into a savings account. Money that does not come home with you is far easier to save and invest.

If you still can not manage to save ten percent of your earnings, there is another means that will help you. It may be necessary to pick up extra hours at work, take on a small second job, or start up a little side business. All of the extra money can be dedicated to making that ten percent minimum savings and investment quota.

Remember to Invest the Money That You Save

Now, once you achieve the monthly goal of setting up a full ten percent or greater of take home pay in savings, you must remember the critical second part of the equation. Just saving the money is not enough to get you financially ahead towards an enjoyable retirement. You need to invest the money in some vehicle or instruments that allow you to compound it at a decent return on your investments.

Finding quality investments that generate passive or residual income is an even better idea. There are various forms of these, ranging from rental investment properties to high paying dividend stocks. Whatever investments that you decide on, they should give you higher returns than the pitifully low interest paying investments like CD's, money markets, and Treasuries are currently yielding.

Should You Invest in Numismatic or Gold and Silver Coins?

So you have at last reached the decision that it is time for you to get involved with gold and silver investments. You waited a few years to have confidence that the precious metals markets were in consistent uptrend modes. This does not mean that you have missed out on all the gains.

Gold and silver have been rising for about ten years now, and they should have another eight to ten years left of the bull market rally in which you can participate. The real question is, in what form of physical gold or silver holdings should you put your hard earned investment money? You have several choices available to you.

Bullion coins and bars or numismatic collectible coins are the most common means for you to acquire physical silver and gold for your investment portfolio. In the subsequent paragraphs, you will understand what these different physical forms of the precious metals are, as well as what their advantages and disadvantages prove to be.

What Are Gold and Silver Bullion?

Gold and silver bullion are either of the two precious metals stored in the forms of bars and ingots or occasionally coins.

Another way of putting this is that bullion does not have any real value other than that of the metals found in it. Buying gold and silver in bullion form means that you will be getting it for the cheapest possible price for the physical metal. This price that you will pay will only involve a very slight premium over the metal value that it contains.

What are Gold and Silver Bullion Bars?

There are many examples of gold and silver bullion. Gold and silver comes in both bullion bars or coins. While silver and even platinum bullion is growing in popularity, gold bullion is still the most beloved and priceless form that investors buy

Bars prove to be a reasonably good choice for investors, though they require you to purchase the metal in larger sized quantities, such as hundreds of ounces for silver, and sometimes even a kilogram, or over thirty-two ounces, for gold. This means that a kilogram bar of gold will run you over $45,000, while a small ten ounce bar will cost you more than $14,000. Even a hundred ounce bar of silver will cost you over $3,000. Because of this higher cost to enter bullion bars, bullion coins prove to be more popular, especially with people who enjoy the feeling of collecting something.

What are Gold and Silver Bullion Coins?

Bullion gold and silver coins are issued by the governments of several countries every year. The United States, Canada, Austria, Australia, South Africa, Mexico, and others mint one ounce and sometimes ten ounce bullion gold and silver coins.

These American Eagles, Canadian Maple Leafs, Austrian Philharmonics, Australian Koalas, South African Krugerrands, and Mexican Peso Centenarios have the advantage of being smaller denominations of gold and silver for you to acquire.

They do come at a slight premium over the spot value of gold and silver. This can range from an extra dollar to four or five dollars per coin for silver, and an extra ten dollars to fifty dollars for gold. Because there is some small collectible value to these coins that come from popular mints, they cost a little bit more. Less popular coins such as the Krugerrand will come at a smaller premium than will more popular coins, such as the Canadian Maple Leaf or American Eagles.

What Are the Downsides to Gold and Silver Bullion Coins?

Like with every thing in life, gold and silver bullion coins have their downside. They are a popular and easy way to store, save, and transport your bullion, but they are not without disadvantages. The main disadvantage centers on the softness of the metals. Gold and silver are softer metals that must be handled with care. Especially when bullion comes in coin format, buyers will expect that you keep them in pristine condition. This means that gold and silver bullion coins that demonstrate signs of scratches, damage, or wear will not be so easy to sell at the price that they typically can command.

Because of this, individual gold and silver bullion coins will require a larger amount of storage space than will comparable precious metal bars. Neither of them requires a lot of room, but if you are dealing with a small safe deposit box, keeping several gold or silver bars will take up less room than dozens or even hundreds of gold or silver bullion coins.

With gold and silver bullion coins, investors should seek out proof quality coins. This is because these are new coins and they are preserved and sold in this mint condition. Investors will definitely frown on bullion coins that are not in well preserved condition.

What Are Gold and Silver Numismatic Coins?

Numismatic coins are a different element altogether. A numismatic coin is one that has some additional collectible value to it besides its inherent gold or silver content. This additional value springs from the rarity and condition of the coin, or sometimes the two factors together. These are also typically historical coins that have not survived in any great quantity. There are many examples of numismatic coins out there, and some coins are only of collectible value if they are both old and well preserved.

As an example, a Morgan Silver dollar from the 1800's from the Carson City mint is rarer than the many common Morgan dollars from the other mints like Philadelphia or San Francisco. It would certainly be a numismatic coin if this hundred plus year old Morgan Silver Dollar bearing the CC mint mark also proved to be in fantastic condition. More common Morgan silver dollars fall in the range of semi-numismatic coins, since they have some small collectible value that sets them apart from the newly minted bullion coins that governments produce every year.

What is the Argument for Buying Gold and Silver Numismatic Coins?

In 1933, President Franklin D. Roosevelt declared holding gold bullion to be illegal. He forced everyone to sell their gold bullion coins to the government at the then current price.

Only holders of numismatic collectible coins proved to be exempt from this order. This is much of the basis for why coin dealers suggest that you purchase numismatic collectible coins as investments. It is important for you to know that there is no law or legally binding statute in effect that states that such coins would ever be exempted in a future potential gold seizure.

Some people also love the thrill of collecting rare and old things. Historical coins are certainly interesting to look at and hold. You can fill a collection with many different themes of gold and silver numismatic coins and make it a hobby.

What is the Downside to Gold and Silver Numismatic Coins?

The downside to these gold and silver collectible coins lies in their premium over spot. You should ask yourself how much more you are willing to pay over the actual price of gold or silver for a given coin. If paying hundreds of dollars extra for a single one ounce gold coin, or paying dozens of dollars more for only a one ounce silver coin is repulsive to you, then you should simply steer clear of this form of gold and silver investing.

Four Places Where You Should Not Get Investment Advice

Everyone today seems to want to offer you investment advice. Anymore, it seems that you do not even have to pay for it to get it. Among the myriads of different groups who give out investment advice for free or for a charge, there are four groups from which you should not take such investment advice at all.

It may surprise you to learn who these four groups are that you should steer clear of when you seek advice for your investments. They are banks, the government, the media, and investment brokers. In the following paragraphs, you will see the reasons why you should avoid them all.

Why You Should Not Seek Investment Advice From Banks

It should not surprise you to learn that banks are not in business to make your life better and more successful. They are not out to make you into a wealthy man or woman. They are looking to make as much money off of your deposits and loans as they legitimately can. This does not mean that banks will intentionally give you bad advice. It is just to say that they are running for profit businesses with their own best interests at heart, and never yours.

With banks, you should let them stick to what they do best. This is safeguarding your money, accounts, and other valuables. They also do not do a bad job when they provide you with home and car loans. But even in these core activities, banks operate with the motive to make profits, not to help you out of the goodness of their hearts.

Why You Should Not Seek Investment Advice From the Government

Here is some more shocking news for you. The government is also not a good place from which to get your investment advice. You might ask why they would not be interested in your success, since they are able to collect taxes on any gains that you make. While this is true, the government actually makes a lot more money off of your sweat and labor than they do off of any investments that you pursue.

They would far rather that you work more and create more highly taxable earnings than that you spend your time investing and garnering returns that they tax at lower capital gains rates.

The other problem with taking investment advice from the government is that they are not famous for running a tight financial ship themselves. Consider that the government has not been able to balance its own books in more than ten years. They run horrific deficits constantly and have the highest national debt in the entire history of the world.

Just look at the state of the finances of Social Security and Medicare.

Not only this, but when they have put their hands into private businesses in the economy, they have mostly mismanaged or further run them into the ground. It is sad to say it, but if the government gives you investment advice, then you should probably try to take the contrarian approach. This means that you would do the opposite of what they were suggesting on purpose.

Why You Should Not Seek Investment Advice From the Media

Hopefully you are not currently making the mistake of many Americans who go to the media for their investment advice. When you smile at this idea, remember Mad Money Jim Cramer. Although you may not take him too seriously, there are millions of Americans who hang on his every cynical word. The problem with the financial media is that they are not in the investment advisory business at all.

Instead, they are in the entertainment business. Media channels, even financial media stations, are entirely about boosting their ratings to generate as high an advertising return as possible. This means that they will do whatever they have to do, and say whatever they have to say, in order to keep you and as many other people watching as they possibly can.

Some of these financial personalities have admitted to as much in little watched interviews. This does not make them bad, or even unethical. It just makes them a terrible place to seriously turn to for good investment advice for your hard earned money and investment portfolio. Do not believe everything that they say, just because they say it on television or the radio. Stick with letting the media entertain you, since this is what they do well.

Why You Should Not Seek Investment Advice From Investment Brokers

This last category may seem like the most ironic one of all. Practically everyone pays investment brokers for much coveted advice on their investment goals and holdings. But even this group is not the one from which you should seek such out such investment advice. You are likely wondering why investment brokers are not a good choice to talk with concerning your investments.

The biggest reason is because they charge exorbitant fees and commissions for any advice that they give you. This is how these brokerage houses not only stay in business, but post increasingly larger profits and pay bigger bonuses to their executives year in and year out. A sampling has been taken of how much money the average client will spend with a brokerage firm on just the typical sized retirement accounts over thirty years.

The results proved to be shocking, showing that more than three hundred thousand dollars are paid between spreads, commissions, and fees that the brokerages exact from the typical client in that amount of time. And this did not even include actively managed accounts.

If the only reason to avoid investment brokers' advice was that it comes dearly, you might manage to justify the cost to yourself. There is another strong reason to avoid them and the suggestions that they peddle. This is that the goal of investment brokers is to keep you invested into a mutual fund or stock as long as possible to help support the prices.

As an example, when was the last time that you heard an investment broker suggest to you that you should sell now and lock in your profits while prices are high?

Instead, they always tell you that you are in this for the long term and you should let them ride until retirement. This is not good investment advice at all. Wealthy people know all too well that there is always a good time to take a profit, and also that there is no such thing as a bad profit in investments.

Finally, remember the scandals that have enveloped even the largest and best known of the investment brokers. Most all of them have been found guilty of pushing investments that they knew were either worthless or highly overrated to their clients. They did this because the financial compensation on such products was simply too lucrative to miss.

From Who Should You Be Getting Your Investment Advice?

The person from who you should be getting your investment advice is you. You must become educated so that you are able to perform your own research. Remember that no one else will ever really have your best interests at heart besides you. You care more about your own money, investments, retirement, and future than all of these other groups discussed above do combined.

Investors May Look For Shorting U.S. Treasury Bonds in 2011

Treasuries are debt obligations that the United States government issues. Among the various types of debt that the government sells to investors like yourself are Treasury Notes, Treasury Bills, and Treasury Bonds.

While the time frames until maturity on Treasury Notes can range from one to ten years and Treasury Bills are issued for less than a year, Treasury Bonds are longer term investments that do not mature for fully thirty years.

Everything that you need to know about an investment idea in 2011 to short Treasury Bonds is explained in the following paragraphs.

What are Treasury Bonds?

It is essential to understand something about Treasury Bonds before you undertake an investment strategy to short them. Treasury bonds represent the longest term debt obligation offered by the United States government. They come with thirty year maturities. These Federal government debt instruments pay you interest when you buy them. The payments are made one time every six months until they reach their maturity. When the time comes for the Treasury Bond to mature, then you will be given its actual face value.

Treasury Bonds can be bought and sold in reasonable increments that the vast majority of investors can afford. These start at only $100 minimum. They go up from there in $100 increments. Single auctions allow investors to purchase even five million dollars in Treasury Bonds in non competitive bids. Competitive bid situations permit you to buy as much as thirty-five percent of an initial offer.

How Do Yields and Prices of Treasury Bonds Relate to One Another?

The reality is that most investors who buy Treasury Bonds do not hold them until the bonds mature unless they are institutions like pensions funds or universities. This is because the yield and price of Treasury bonds can change. They are set at regular auctions that the Treasury holds in order to sell these bonds. The price can turn out to be equal to, higher, or lower than the bond's actual face value. These bonds are initially sold at the price determined at auction in the Treasury Direct online program, or by dealers, brokers, and banks after auction.

Prices of Treasury Bonds after this point are determined by the rising and falling interest rate yields that come with them. The yields and values of Treasury Bonds are inverse to each other, like with other kinds of bonds. This simply means that when the interest rates go up, then the prices, or values, of these Treasury Bonds fall. If interest rates fall, then the values of the Treasury Bonds rise. So when you hear the tip to short Treasury Bonds, the idea is that interest rates will rise, causing the prices of the bonds to go down. A person who is short Treasury Bonds when the prices fall can potentially make a great amount of money.

How Have Treasury Bonds Performed in the Past?

In the past several years since 2006, Treasury Bonds have done very well for investors who owned them. This is because the demand for Treasuries sky-rocked when investors sought safe places to park their money in the wake of the financial crisis that began in 2007. This created great demand for Treasury Bonds that drove up their prices and values.

Not only this, but the Federal Reserve had to cut interest rates aggressively for several years. Each time that they cut the rates, the inverse relationship between yields and prices caused the value of the Treasuries to rise. Any investors who owned Treasury Bonds watched the value of their government bond holdings rise substantially as the Fed lowered the national interest rates from nearly five percent to almost zero percent.

Why Were Treasury Bonds Relatively Risk Free?

Until the Fed began cutting interest rates, these rates sat at a level that was at or above the national average for several decades. This meant that it was unlikely that the Fed would choose to increase rates. Since the Federal Reserve proved to be unlikely to raise the rates, then the chances of the inversely related prices of the bonds going down were low. This made Treasury Bonds almost risk free for many years.

Besides this, the Federal Debt was still manageable in the 1990's up through the start of the financial crisis. There was almost no chance that the government would find itself unable to find enough buyers to finance the debt and interest payments. As these bonds are guaranteed by the full faith and credit of the Federal government, risks of default or forbearance were next to nothing.

What Has Changed with Regards to Treasury Bonds?

Several things have changed with Treasury Bonds that makes them a better opportunity sell short, or own in negative quantities, than to buy them. Interest rates are as low as they can go now. This means that they can only stay the same or go up from this level of from zero to point twenty-five percent where they sit presently. As the interest rates rise, then the value of the Treasury Bonds will go down, according to the inverse relationship between yields and values.

The other possibility is of course that the massive amount of debt that the Treasury needs to finance will prove to be more than they can accomplish at these lower interest rates. There are many economists who speculate that this will prove to be an increasingly big problem for the Federal government that is paying so little interest on such a large amount of long term debt. As demand is softer for the Treasury Bonds, or as their interest rates are forced to go higher at auctions, then the prices will fall. This is yet another compelling reason to set up a trade to short U.S. Treasury Bonds in 2011.

How Do You Short Treasury Bonds?

In order to short bonds, you are basically borrowing them from a holder of the bond and then selling them in the market for the current price. You do this in an investment brokerage account. Whether the price rises against you or declines in your favor, you will eventually have to buy back the exact same bond that you sold in order to return it to the group from which you borrowed it earlier. You pay a small fee to borrow the bond.

You are also responsible for any interest payments that come due to the owner of the bond.

Shorting the bond is exactly the opposite of purchasing it when you believe that lower yields will result. The reason that you want to do it now is that the rates simply have to go higher soon, for one of the reasons just discussed.

How Much Money Can You Make By Shorting U.S. Treasury Bonds?

The answer to how much money that you can make by shorting U.S. Treasury bonds is one that may surprise you. The fact is that the limit to your profits is the distance from the price that you short it at all the way to zero. This is a hypothetical point, since Treasury Bonds would not decline to zero unless the government defaulted on them.

But as interest rates get higher and higher, the values of these bonds will go lower and lower. Given the scenario of potentially sharply higher interest rates in the future, would you rather be long or short Treasury Bonds this year?

The Three Major Lessons I Learned From Investing in Silver

Investing in silver is an exciting and rewarding area with which to get involved. This last year alone, silver is up more than seventy-five percent.

It would be a mistake to think that investing in silver is necessarily easy and nothing but nonstop one directional gains.

The truth is that silver - like all investments - has its ups and downs all the while it is moving in a general uptrend. There are three lessons that I learned when I started investing in silver that can benefit you and save you a painful and steep learning curve. You will read about these in the subsequent paragraphs.

Lesson Number One - Be Careful with Leverage

Leverage is the ability to multiply the purchasing power of your money when you actually buy an investment. With precious metals, you are capable of leveraging anywhere from two to one to twenty-five to one your investment dollars, depending on the investment vehicle that you utilize. Now, this may have you wide eyed with wild excitement at the thought of how much money that you can make if you can buy ten thousand dollars of silver with only a thousand dollars of your own money.

The problem with this amount of leverage is that silver does not move up in a straight line. If you buy it and then it pulls back on a significant correction, then you can suffer such terrible losses that you are forced out of your positions at a crushing loss. Consider my example before you jump all over the leverage train with silver. I had a margin account that I set up with Monex Depository. They permitted me to buy one bar of silver in cash and to leverage three more bars with margin.

So long as silver held level, this was not a problem. The dilemma arose when silver dropped five dollars per ounce on a severe pull-back. This represented an over twenty percent correction. Because the value of my additional three leveraged bars of silver was down so steeply, I was forced to sell one of the bars at a terrible loss.

Later this same year, silver took off, and it is about to finish the year up over seventy-five percent higher. My remaining three bars are up nicely, but I still got badly burned in a year when silver posted a phenomenal return.

This happened to me with only four to one leverage in silver. If you had owned silver at a higher leverage of ten to one or even greater, then you likely would have been forced out of the entire investment at a total loss of your original investment dollars. This is why you have to be so careful with leverage, especially higher amounts of leverage.

Only small moves become exaggerated by the power of leverage. This can make you a tremendous amount of money when silver prices directly move your way, and it can also cost you dearly if they move against you over the short term.

Lesson Number Two - Be Patient

Another critical lesson that I learned in my silver investing is that you have to be patient when you pursue this type of investment. Silver does not always make dramatic moves in your favor. Just because you have bought it on a pullback does not mean that it will take right back off. The truth is that sometimes nothing meaningful happens in the silver price for even weeks at a time.

Other times, you will buy into the gray metal and then the price will seem to immediately begin going down. You can quickly be under water with this investment and that can not cause you to panic. When you are holding a negative position with your new silver investment, you will just have to be patient and wait for the price of silver to come back. Depending on how far down the price goes after you buy it, this could require months or even a year's worth of time before the price moves back to the level at which you purchased it.

This is why investing in silver is not for the panicky or the faint of heart. If you are a person who bites your nails with every tick that an investment makes against you, then you should be very careful with investing in silver in the first place. Silver proves to be the most volatile of all precious metals. This stems from the small amount of silver that is actually available to be traded on the investment markets.

When you are going to invest in silver for the medium to long term time frame, then you will certainly have to be patient. If you can not stand being in the red for even a few weeks or months, then you should look into some other less volatile investment.

At the very least, you should only buy as much silver as you have cash for, so that you will not watch your losses become multiplied by the double edged sword of leverage. There is no sense in losing sleep at night over an investment.

Lesson Number Three - Conquer Your Greed

When you are making investments in silver, you will also need to learn how to conquer your greed. This is certainly a case of easier to say than to do. Greed, like many of the human vices, is both powerful and ingrained deep into our beings.

You may be wondering what greed has to do with making an investment in silver. Greed is the one factor that stops you and everyone else from cashing out on an investment position once it is in profits. This can seem to have a positive result, especially if the investment continues to go your way. Unfortunately, if the investment goes from profitable to a losing position, then it is a terrible consequence. This happens to investors all of the time.

The lesson to take away from the vice of greed is that if your silver investment is in profits, then you should not end up with a losing position in it later. While you wait for it to go up even more, silver may instead begin a correction that wipes out all of your hard won gains and takes you months to get back into profits. The old saying that there is no such a thing as a bad profit is especially true with silver investments. Fight to overcome your own personal greed.

One way that you can do this is to set a reasonable goal at which point you will sell your silver investment. You would do this before you buy the silver. It might be that you say when silver is up ten or fifteen percent from your entry point that you will agree to sell your position and take your profits.

There is no reason that you might not re-enter silver again later when the price pulls back and corrects temporarily. Just because you take a profit now does not mean that you will never become involved with silver again at some other point in the future. It just means that you will lock in your gains and have something to show for your time and trouble.

Do Commodity ETF's Effect Commodities Prices?

If you have followed commodity prices over the last several years, then you will recognize that they have been steadily rising since they plummeted along with most every other asset in the financial crisis.

There have been various explanations given for this. Some claim that natural demand from around the world explains it.

Others blame hedge funds for the higher prices that threaten to cause inflation. While all of these may play a role, the factor that has changed in the last few years is the effect created by ETF's, or exchange traded funds. In the subsequent paragraphs, you will see why this reason is the better explanation for higher commodity prices than all of the other possibilities that analysts give you.

Supply and Demand Factors

The reason that the government and analysts are closely examining commodity prices in recent months is because they are beginning to show signs that they will lead the threat of inflation in the coming years. Commodities turn out to be an easy arena to learn about supply and demand. While the supply of various commodities has not changed appreciably since 2008, something certainly has.

Gold prices are up over twenty percent, while silver has risen over seventy-five percent so far in 2010. Other commodities are similarly higher, though with less significant gains to show. Since the supply factors have not changed appreciably, it has to be demand that is causing these prices to move sharply higher. The question then is from where is the demand coming?

Does Consumption Demand Explain All of the Rise in Commodities Prices?

Many analysts blame the normal demand from consumers in some countries around the world for the sharply higher prices. It is true that China and other developing economies are demanding greater amounts of commodities.

Still, demand in the United States and other Western countries is flat to lower these past several years. This helps to offset the demand created by the developing countries. The boost in the industrial demand of certain commodities like lead, zinc, copper, and silver is not much greater than it was in the past few years. The growth percentages in such commodities have mostly been level for a number of years now. Demand from the rising economic power houses is simply not enough to explain the rise in prices.

Does Hedge Fund and Commodity Trading Explain the Gains in Commodities Prices?

Other regulators and government agencies are quick to point to and blame hedge funds as the perpetrators of higher commodities prices in the world economy. It is an unusual thing to blame them for all of the price rises, since hedge funds will take both sides of trades on commodities.

Speculators are only performing their market functions when they buy and sell commodities. They may be taking larger long positions than they are short ones, but this is still not sufficient to explain away such dramatic moves in commodities prices over the last few years. They simply do not have the power to take commodities so much higher so quickly.

How Does Government's Fiscal and Monetary Policy Contribute to Higher Commodities Prices?

The United States government has been on a money printing spree since 2008. In the last three years, the Federal Reserve and Treasury have managed to radically grow the supply of American dollar by more than three hundred percent. This is a shocking number that is having a tremendous influence on the psychology of even the average investor on the street. It has created a very real fear of inflation that is gnawing at the minds of common Americans.

In the past, ordinary American investors also feared inflationary policies that the government pursued. Back in those crises, such investors did not have easy access to hard assets like commodities. While there were always the commodities pits of the Chicago Mercantile Exchange and similar commodities and futures exchanges, these types of investments have never managed to break through to reach the average American investor. Some other vehicle has to explain how the common American investor has found a way to bid up the commodities complex more than only professional investors have done.

Exchange Traded Funds and The Role That They Play in Higher Commodities Prices

In the last few years, a new investment has become increasingly more visible and popular. These are the exchange traded funds. Exchange traded funds are investments that trade on the stock market exchanges exactly like a stock. They are easily bought and sold in any stock investment account. They trade with great volume and frequency all day long so long as the exchanges are open. This makes them easily accessible, familiar feeling, and safe to the typical American investor in a way that commodities exchanges never have been.

There are literally hundreds of commodities exchange traded funds available now. Barclays of Great Britain and American investment banking giant Morgan Stanely began a partnership a few years ago that saw more than forty of them launched under the iShares brand name at a single time. With such mainstream and familiar players involved in exchange traded funds, this has also contributed to the willingness and ability of Americans to become involved in commodities in a major way.

The difference now is that as commodities rose in the past, the majority of these commodities' exchange traded funds simply did not exist. But since 2005, it has become increasingly easy for financial advisers and retail American investors to move their money into commodities via these exchange traded funds found on both the American and London exchanges.

Proof of how large commodities under management are growing is easy to find. Barclays reported back in November that these commodities being managed had risen by $19 billion to a new high of $340 billion in October. The growth is especially attributed to investments linked to indexes like exchange traded funds.

These exchange traded funds explain the dramatic rise in commodities prices, particularly in gold and silver. People like you view these two precious metals most of all as safe places to hide their money when they fear inflation will be created by the irresponsible actions and failed policies of the United States government.

In the past, it required a lot of effort to take positions in these commodities, even though gold and silver can be acquired in coin and bullion form. Now you have an easy entrance to these commodities and even more exotic ones like timber, copper, oil, zinc, lead, cotton, and wheat using exchange traded funds.

Exchange traded funds are a popular and increasingly beloved way to invest your money into hard assets like gold and silver. The problem with this growing practice is that it is significantly impacting the prices of commodities in general. This in turns leads to inflation, as the costs of various end user goods and even food rise along with the prices of inputs. It also causes the dollar to decline more and faster since most commodities are still priced in U.S. dollars.

So while it is good for investors to have choices for places to put their money, there are real world consequences of these investments that they are making today that will impact the prices that everyone pays tomorrow.

Why You Should Not Invest To Be Secure And Comfortable

You may have never stopped to consider the reasons that motivate people to invest. Investing is often motivated by emotions rather than by truly logical and thought out reasons.

You first probably invest in order to be secure. After that, you may think to invest in order to be comfortable. Finally, you will have somewhere in mind that you should invest to become wealthy. This is the way that most people approach investing.

Unfortunately this is the wrong order entirely. You should be investing first to be wealthy, then so that you can be comfortable, and finally so that you can be secure. The investor psychology for investing is considered in the following paragraphs.

Why You Should Not Invest to Be Secure

There is nothing wrong with your desire to be secure. Security brings comfort, peace, and even a good night's rest. The problem with security is that it does not make a good mentality and motivation for investing. The search for security leads you to avoid risk. It will help you in your quest to find a job that enables you to pay your bills. It does not aid you in making investments.

Investing is not a practice that you should pursue in the effort to feel secure. Investing comes with risk, no matter how conservative the investment proves to be.

If you think to invest in order to improve your security, then you must think very long term. In the short run, investing will not improve your security. Working so that you can earn income will. This is why investing in order to feel secure is not a good idea. It should not be your first consideration at all, but rather it ought to be your final one.

Why You Should Not Invest to be Comfortable

If you are like most people, then the thought of living a comfortable life really appeals to you. This is only a natural human impulse. What people would not want to live an easy life where they did not have to work, surrounded by all of the creature comforts imaginable?

Once again, comfort is not an ideal characteristic for investing. If you are comfortable, then you will quickly find that you will not have much in the way of motivation and energy in order to invest and strive towards becoming rich. People who are satisfied, and even happy, where they are in life, simply do not have any drive or real desire to improve their condition.

It is you who are dissatisfied with where you are in life who will stand up and do something to improve it. This is something that you should remember. There is nothing wrong with enjoying your life. A fine line exists between a life where you feel good, and a life where you are so comfortable that you do not wish to change anything about it.

Another problem with investing with the mentality of becoming comfortable lies in the fact that investing is often not comfortable, nor does it lead to ease and repose. Investing involves wrestling with different choices of investments in order to come up with the best ones. Not only this, but once you are invested, you have to constantly be on top of your investments in order to make sure that the factors that surround them have not changed.

An investment that is a good idea today may be a poor one tomorrow. At the very least, you always need to read to stay abreast of the trends that your investment involves. If you become comfortable, you will not have the impetus to seriously pursue the effort and study that you need to do to continue to invest successfully.

You have never heard that investing is comfortable and easy. This is the reason that you should not invest with a primary motivation of being comfortable. Besides this, if you spend all of your time, efforts, and energy on reaching the goal of becoming comfortable, then you will find that you do not have much of these components left for the primary purpose of investing, which is to become wealthy.

Why You Should Invest to be Wealthy

The right motivation for investing is not to be secure. It is also not to be comfortable. If this comes as a surprise to you, then you will likely be wondering what is the proper incentive for investing. What should you be focused on in your efforts to invest? The answer is simple. You should invest with the ultimate goal to grow wealthy.

Building up wealth does not happen overnight. This is a long term goal that will require careful and determined investing.

It is not easy, and you should not expect it to be a simple thing. Still, it is the proper motivation for investing. Investing to be wealthy is not a goal that you will quickly and easily achieve and that will leave you feeling like you do not have to work towards it anymore. This is why it is a better motivation for you than is investing to be secure or investing to be comfortable.

One thing that the rich generally have in common is that they are never satisfied with where they are. They are always seeking to improve and to increase their assets, investments, and holdings to a greater level.

There is a famous story of a very wealthy man who had achieved everything in his life. He had built up an enormous international business. He had amassed a tremendous personal fortune. He was already considered to be among the wealthiest, if not the richest, men in American history. When the man was interviewed about his ambitions and achievements, the reporter asked him when he would be satisfied and when he would have achieved enough wealth. His curt answer may surprise you. He said, just a little bit more.

This story is true of the majority of rich people in America today. Just because they have gained great wealth does not mean that they are satisfied. They continue to work and strive to invest wisely and properly so that they can maintain what they have and build up still more.

This should be your goal as well. You should invest with the motivation of growing rich. When you do this, keep in mind that this is a goal for which you can mark milestones. Yet it should not ever be one that you have fully achieved and stop working towards.

When you become too comfortable and secure, it is easy to stop caring about making progress in life. A person who is not engaged in the pursuit of something is already dead.

You should first focus on building up your wealth. Once you do this, you will be able to have a comfortable life around it and to secure it. It is easy to think about all of the things that you can do once you are rich, comfortable and secure. Instead, why not think today about how you will practically reach your goal of becoming wealthy?

The Difference Between An Inside And An Outside Investor

You may not realize this, but most books that are written for investors are actually created to help outside investors. The overwhelming majority of people fall into this category. You are probably an outside investor yourself.

The main problem with this is that the investors who generally make the most money are usually the inside investors. An inside investor is not the same thing as an inside trader, who engages in illegal actions to make money with illicitly obtained knowledge. The ins and outs of an inside investor are explained in the subsequent paragraphs, along with the differences between these inside investors and outside investors.

What Is An Inside Investor Exactly?

An investor who is an insider is someone who has control over a company's direction. An outside investor does not have this kind of control. Inside investors are literally on the investment's inside. This means that they exert some form of control over the direction of the company and its management. This does not mean that they will have total control over the company. It only means that they will have some form of major influence and control over the management.

Inside investors literally speaking are a director of a company or a corporate officer. They can also be someone who owns at least ten percent of the stock's shares. All of these are inside investors. Investors who are able to invest on the inside as opposed to from the outside always have a huge advantage. They are able to increase their returns in the investment and to reduce their risk for one thing.

What Is an Outside Investor?

An outside investor is a person who owns shares in a company's stock but is not in any way able to control the direction or management of the company. As you do not have control over what is happening, you as an outside investor are entrusting your money to the officers of the company. It is up to them to make wise decisions that effectively grow the value of the company and increase its stock price so that you as a partial owner, albeit an outsider, can benefit from your investment growing.

Inside investors possess three characteristics that outside investors simply do not. They have a great amount of education financially. They claim a wealth of experience. Besides this, they often have extra cash to invest.

What Specific Controls Does an Inside Investor Gain Over An Investment?

Outside investors have no actual control over the company in which they invest. It is true that they can vote in the shareholder's meetings, but this does not make any practical difference. Really their only power is to sell the investment if they are unhappy with its performance.

You can sharply contrast this with the control that an inside investor has over an investment. They control the income and expenses along with assets and liability ratios. They have direct control over the investment's management. They also can determine how the taxes are figured up and paid.

Inside investors control all agreements' terms and conditions. They have influence over the timing and characteristics of the investment as well. Besides this, they have power over the information released on the investment and the general access to it. It really is astonishing how much power you gain over an investment when you are an inside investor.

Can A Person Without Enormous Wealth Become an Inside Investor?

It is interesting to note that you do not have to be a high net worth individual or a person with a large amount of income in order to be an inside investor. There are other ways to become an inside investor. If you are an individual who possesses a strong financial education but lacks the significant financial resources of a well accredited investor, then you can still attain the privileged and lucrative status of inside investor.

You do this by starting and building up your own company. As you run the company, eventually sell it, or take it public, then you are exerting the management control over your investment that makes you an inside investor. This is the means that many individuals use to get into inside investments in a personal and powerful way today.

Another way to become an inside investor is to gain the ten percent threshold of shares in a smaller company.

Such companies are almost exclusively where all the major gains are to be found in investments. James O'Shaughnessy's book "What Works On Wall Street" has found that small capitalization stocks almost always massively outperform the other levels of stocks.

In fact, practically all of the best returns to be realized from investing in companies are found in the categories of micro capitalization stocks that have tiny market capitalization of less than twenty-five million dollars. It is hard to get into such companies for most investors, since mutual funds do not invest in such small outfits, and these little companies that feature high growth are hard for you and for practically everyone else to find. Some people become inside investors by acquiring the ten percent or more of shares in these companies.

If you are unable to locate such companies in which you can invest, then you can always build up your own small capitalization company and stock. This way, you will have total control or near total control over the destiny of your investment. The key advantage to this is that the risk levels are substantially reduced as you gain more control over your investment.

What Are The Different Ways that Inside Investors Obtain Control Over Investments?

There are two main ways that outside investors gain control over investments. They can create it. This is done by starting your own business. You put your own capital at risk and are both owner and manager of the business. You might have outside investors who trust you to run the company well. Your responsibility to them will be a fiduciary one. You will be expected to manage their share of the investment effectively.

In the process, you can control your own investment's destiny for your ultimate benefit. You will also have privileged insider information access, since you are the owner and manager of the investment.

The other way that you can become an outside investor is to buy control over a business as an investment. You do not have to acquire full ownership in the existing company to achieve this. You only need to gain a controlling interest in it. You can do this by acquiring a majority of the stock shares. The more investor controls you gain as the inside investor, the better and more effectively you will diminish your investment risk.

This takes skill to manage the investment and company well. Being an outside investor is about more than just having money and control over the company and investment. Given what you know about inside versus outside investors now, which type of investor would you rather be?

What Are The Major Advantages to Exchange Traded Funds?

If you follow the markets much or listen to financial news television, then you have heard the expression ETF, or Exchange Traded Funds. Exchange Traded Funds are an investment vehicle that you have seen grow in popularity dramatically in the last ten years.

As they provide you with a unique investment vehicle that is both similar to and yet distinctly different from mutual funds and stocks, they are something that you should understand.

The following paragraphs go through the main concepts of ETF's and why they are a different and interesting investment product.

What Exactly Are Exchange Traded Funds?

Exchange Traded Funds prove to be investment funds that actually trade on the major stock exchanges. They can be easily bought and sold during the day, which makes them like stocks. Unlike stocks, they contain a number of assets like bonds, stocks, or commodities. Their value turns out to be about the same as the underlying assets' net asset value.

Their price is based on this net asset value. This makes them like mutual funds. An easy one line explanation of Exchange Traded Funds is that they are index funds that investors buy and sell on the significant stock exchanges.

These funds have become the most heavily traded and beloved kind of exchange traded product available.

How Did Exchange Traded Funds Arise?

In light of their popularity, it may surprise you to learn that Exchange Traded Funds are actually a fairly new concept and product. These mostly index based investment funds have only existed within the United States since 1993. They did not reach European markets until 1999. A joint venture between MSCI, a distribution company Funds Distributor, Inc, and BGI created the very first Exchange Traded Funds that were specific to different countries back in 1993.

Barclays Bank became involved in the Exchange Traded Funds market in 1996 and with their partner and fund index provider Morgan Stanley, they revolutionized the ETF concept. Over time, this product morphed into the popular and well known exchange traded funds brand iShares that are a household name to investors around the world. Barclays renamed the WEBS as iShares MSCI Index Fund Shares, and they rapidly grew from seventeen country tracking indexes into the scores of them available today. These funds offered smaller investors the opportunity to become involved in foreign markets and exchanges.

The individual S&P Sector Spiders that track the nine segments of the popular index were launched by State Street Global Advisers in 1998. That same year, the Dow Diamonds that tracked the well known Dow Jones Industrial Average began trading. Another landmark in Exchange Traded Funds was the NASDAQ index tracking Exchange Traded Fund, called cubes. They track the NASDAQ 100 exchange.

Barclays boosted its Exchange Traded Funds efforts in the iShares line up in the year 2000 by launching a large number of them all in one year. They popularized ETF's at this point by pouring a great amount of effort and time into educating and reaching long term investors with the products. It took only five years for these iShares Exchange Traded Funds to overtake all rivals in both the United States and Europe. This leading Exchange Traded Fund family has possessed more assets and varieties than all competitors ever since.

For the most of their history, Exchange Traded Funds have been exclusively index funds. A few years ago in 2008, the SEC Securities and Exchange Commission started to approve the development and deployment of Exchange Traded Funds that are actively managed. This marks a real break from Exchange Traded Funds in the past that were passively managed to follow a given index.

In the last decade, Exchange Traded Funds have multiplied. Nowadays, you can find ones that follow particular sectors of the markets; regions of the world; types of bonds; futures; commodities like gold, silver, copper, wheat; and various other classes of assets. To illustrate how popular and numerous they have become, in September of 2010, nine hundred and sixteen different Exchange Traded Funds existed. They contained a combined eight hundred and eighty two billion dollars in total assets. This proved to be more than one hundred and eighty nine billion dollars more than in the year before.

What Are The Major Advantages to Exchange Traded Funds?

Exchange Traded Funds can provide you with some tremendous advantages over stocks and mutual funds. Naturally, this will depend on what your investment objectives are.

If you are interested in becoming invested in the stock market on a diversified basis both rapidly and with low fees, then they are the way to go. For practicality and efficiency of buying into the stock market, no vehicles can compare or compete with them. If you are looking for a way to purchase a specific type of asset class or sector, they are also your best vehicle. Their fees average a mere .9% in entry costs, compared with mutual funds 1.6% typical amount.

Why are Exchange Traded Funds Different Than Stocks?

Stocks represent an investment and partial ownership in a single company. Exchange Traded Funds commonly hold dozens, or in some cases, even hundred of different companies' stocks. This gives them a distinct advantage in diversifying your investments that stocks simply can not provide.

For example, if you wanted to create a holding of a great number of small American companies, or alternatively for large American companies, you could buy many different stocks, one at a time. This would require a great amount of investment, possibly in the tens of thousands of dollars. You would also be forced to pay transaction costs on each individual stock. The cost for you as an individual investor would be crippling. But thanks to Exchange Traded Funds you are able to do this with only a single ETF investment.

You pay only one fee to buy and one to sell. With a single Exchange Traded Fund, you can control a significant number of stocks, all at once. You can acquire these on all of the major stock market averages, for international stocks, real estate investment trusts, and even gold and silver. Think of any publicly traded class and you can almost be sure that there will be an Exchange Traded Fund available for it.

Why are Exchange Traded Funds Different Than Mutual Funds?

Exchange Traded Funds are substantially different from mutual funds, even though they have some similarities. Both of them hold collections of investments. Some exchange traded funds are even set up in similar formats as mutual funds. This is where the commonalities end.

Exchange Traded Funds are substantially different in other ways. These ETF's trade all day long, like stocks. Mutual funds only allow you to buy in or cash out after the market has closed. This is because mutual funds will take orders throughout the normal Wall Street day, but they will not know their net asset value until the market closes. They pay out based on the final prices of all the stocks or bonds within the fund at the close of the day.

Exchange Traded Funds also offer tax advantages that mutual funds do not. They can be purchased on margin. Options trade on them and permit you to set up various complicated hedging strategies that you can not do with mutual funds.

What are the Predictions for Silver Prices in 2011?

Gold and silver have just finished phenomenal years for the tenth year in a row. Gold has recorded gains of over twenty-five percent in 2010. Silver blew away its past performance and that of every other asset class with gains that exceeded seventy percent in 2010.

Now that the New Year holiday is behind us, you may be wondering what the brokerages, economists, and major investors are saying about gold and silver prices for 2011 and the coming years. The answer may surprise you, as the experts continue to trip over each other in their efforts to raise their full year and future gold and silver price targets.

Where Do Gold and Silver Start out the New Year?

Gold began the first trading day of the new year 2011 with its all time high once again within the sights. It surpassed $1,420 per ounce in the New York and London Spot markets, only a mere percent away from its record highs. Silver also broke a thirty year peak on this day as it climbed to over $36 per ounce and blew away its previous $30.75 high of thirty years.

The two metals are being solidly supported by fears of possible inflation in the developing and developed economies of the world, by anticipation of additional negative news on the debt in shaky Euro zone countries, and by a growing focus on the unsustainable United States deficit.

The senior analyst at Richcomm Global Services of Dubai claimed that new highs in gold are likely this coming year following the calm period in gold trading during the Christmas and New Years' holidays. The first target is set in the range of $1,455 to $1,480 according to technical levels, he said. This is because the fear factors that are rallying gold and silver are all still intact.

There are doubt and uncertainty over macro economic policies, worry about the stability of currencies, inflation concerns for the medium time frame because of Quantitative Easing II, low interest rates, tensions surrounding Iran and North Korea, and of course risk of additional sovereign debt problems around the developed world.

What Are the Predictions for Gold Prices in 2011?

The range of predictions for gold prices varies by hundreds of dollars for 2011. The majority of forecasters are calling for significantly higher prices though. One long time legendary gold trader, investor, and broker-dealer who advised the Hunt Brothers on their famous efforts to corner the silver market in the 1980s and who helped the government unravel their positions after they were banned is Jim Sinclair.

For going on five years now, Jim Sinclair has been stating that gold will reach $1,650 per ounce in January of 2011.

His prior price target of $1,225 proved to be within a dollar of the actual high that you saw before gold retraced and then continued its relentless march forward. While he may be off by a matter of months on his ultimate call for gold in January, the chances are very good that he will be correct for the overall year of 2011.

Goldman Sachs is another well respected source that has suggested higher gold prices are in the cards in 2011. They have boosted their price targets for many metal based commodities, including copper, silver, and gold. Previously, they had average prices for the year set at $1,325 for 2011 and $1,200 in 2012. They have increased these amounts to $1,575 average yearly prices for both 2011 and 2012 recently.

Goldman's price averages would see gold up over thirteen percent in 2011, depending on how high it reached. Goldman Sachs is among the most profitable investment banks in the world, with a track record of making money that you even saw continue during the dark years of the financial crisis from 2007-2010.

Citibank has a well staffed and respected investment advisory branch called CitiFx Techs. They just released their Twelve Charts of Christmas piece. In this, they called for substantially higher oil and gold prices. They anticipate that gold will rise to $1,700 per ounce this very year. This represents a potential gain of seventeen percent on the year. In the future, they expect to see it trade at $2,000 per ounce.

Other investors and economists are calling for gold to rise to even higher levels this next year and the following years. Martin Armstrong has been named the economist of the year for the U.S. in the past. He sees gold rising to over $5,000 per ounce in the next few years. This would represent gains of over two hundred fifty percent if it materializes.

An institutional investor who fears that hyperinflation is sure to strike the developed world economies is Egon von Greyerz, the head of Matterhorn Asset Management. While he does not give out a specific target for 2011 right now, he does expect to see realistic targets for gold prices in the next several years that will range from $6,000 to $11,000 each ounce. His reasoning for this is spelled out in his recent piece called "Hyperinflation Will Drive Gold to Unthinkable Heights." Here he explains that numerous indicators are pointing to the beginnings of a new ear of hyperinflation in the developed world.

Among his reasons are the fiscal gap is growing at shocking and frightening levels in a number of the world's major economies, the rise of long term interest rates, the currencies that are declining, and the major precious metals making multi year and all time highs as measured against the majority of currencies. He argues that because of this, investors will trip over one another to get into physical silver and gold in order to not lose as much as one hundred percent of the buying power of their cash. Egon von Greyerz is quick to point out that having your own supply of gold and silver is the greatest proven way to protect your wealth from both hyperinflation and deflationary collapses.

What are the Predictions for Silver Prices in 2011?

Silver prices are more difficult to forecast. The other precious metal is incredibly undervalued on a historical comparison basis. It is even undervalued when you measure it up to gold. Besides this, many of the forecasters and their silver price predictions have already been surpassed in just the last month of December and early January. Consider that Morgan Stanley has a projection for average silver prices out in the low $20 range while silver is trading at over $30 per ounce at the very beginning of 2011.

The investment bank Scotia Capital is based in Canada. They recently increased their target prices for silver from $21 per ounce to $26 per ounce. Even their near term peak of $30 per ounce has already been broken in the first trading days of the year. Their high of $35 in the coming year to two is still a reasonable prediction that represents a potential thirteen percent move from current prices.

GFMS is a London based investment consulting service. They expect to see silver prices topping thirty dollars per ounce this year. Once again, their prediction has already been trumped. Considering how fast and high silver has already moved at the end of 2010 and beginning of 2011, you should ask yourself how high you think it might go this year?

<u>MINDSET</u>

"Changing Habits, Attitudes and Intentions"

Mindset

Mindset

Coupon Clipping - The Art of Living Below Your Means

You may be like many people who discovered after the hard times created by the financial crisis and Great Recession that learning to live below your means is not just optional any longer.

With so many people unemployed, the lost art of coupon clipping is again rising in prominence as people struggle to stretch their meager paychecks.

While there is nothing inherently wrong with wanting to save money, living below your means will not get you ahead. The subsequent paragraphs discuss the reasons that you must not focus your time and efforts on spending less, but instead on proactively making more money.

Coupon Clipping Is a Waste of Both Your Time and Energy

Unless you are very accomplished at finding coupons for your weekly needs at the grocery store, you will discover that several hours a week can be involved in going through magazines or on-line coupon websites. You will have to spend more than just a considerable amount of time looking for deals on the things that you need.

On top of this, you will waste a great amount of your personal energy that is lost in the frustrating process. If coupon clipping is taking you two hours or three per week, then you are looking at a good eight to twelve hours per month that you could be using to improve your financial situation. No matter how hard you try at it, coupon clipping will not get you materially ahead, even when it does manage to save you twenty to thirty percent off of your grocery budget each week.

Living Below Your Means Leads to Nowhere

The secret to building up wealth is not in pinching pennies until they scream. When you manage to cut every possible corner in order to save a few dollars, this is not improving your mentality to be successful or to grow wealth. It might keep you from going into debt, but living below your means will not solve your financial problems any more than spending the time and effort to clip coupons will.

Struggling to Save Money Distracts You From The Real Problem

The problem that you have is not necessarily that live too large or spend too much money on things. This is a false understanding of what your dilemma really is. Your real problem with money is that you do not have enough of it coming in every month. Clipping coupons and living below your means will help you to live on what you have in available monthly income, but it will only distract you from the real dilemma. It is critically important that you change your mentality to start focusing on dealing with your actual problem.

Focusing on the Problem Instead of the Solution Does Make Things Worse

Another thing to keep in mind as you are examining your finances is that you must not become consumed with concentrating on the problem regarding your income. The problem is clearly that you do not have enough of this money to go around. Wringing your hands and thinking of ways to stretch your limited dollars is only focusing on the problem at hand. Instead, you have to realize what the solution to this problem is so that you can begin to concentrate your efforts to address this.

Focusing on the Problem Keeps You in a State of Poverty

One thing that separates the wealthy from the rest of us is their attitude about their financial situation. They have an extremely positive, can do financial mentality. Notice that you do not ever see the Donald Trumps of the world wring their hands and clip coupons. They never did this, even before they became fantastically wealthy.

A wealthy person never concentrated his or her mind on why they are poor and what they can do to be less poor. Instead, they looked around at ways that they could increase their income, savings, and investments.

The Solution Is to Find Ways and Means of Increasing Your Income

Do you remember those ten or more hours per month that you spend to find, clip, and use coupons at the grocery store? This is a significant amount of time that you might put to more practical use.

If you used the ten hours per month on a solution to increase your income, then you would be far better off than with the coupons. Coupons never solved any individual's or family's financial problems. An extra job or small side business can help.

When you work an extra job ten to twenty hours a week, it may not be the most fun activity that you can think of, but it is certainly a more proactive way to build up wealth than when you clip coupons and watch every cent that you possibly spend. Not only this, but it will give you a sense of satisfaction that you are doing something to actually improve your financial state.

The saying that the best defense is a good offense applies to your finances as well.

Alternatively, you might find some side business that you could start. There are many Internet based business ideas these days that permit you to generate a second income with only a small amount of time commitment and work put in to the project. Maybe you are a person who loves writing. You might write articles for any number of article based site such as eHow, Ezine, or TextBrokers. Perhaps you are an individual with a talent for making small handicraft items.

These are always popular when sold at festivals or over the Internet. You might get involved with auctions like on eBay. If you are someone who is good with book knowledge, you could become a tutor for one of the many online tutor companies, like Tutor.com. If you enjoy taking pictures, there are stock photo websites that you can sell them on, like Fotolia, Inmagine, and Photos.com. The possibilities for Internet based businesses are as many and varied as your imagination will let them be.

What You Should Do After You Have Additional Money Coming In

Once you have either begun a little side business or found another job to bring in more money, then you can really compound your efforts by finding some residual, passive income producing investments where you can put this money to work. Not everyone will have the money to buy an investment property and rent it out to tenants.

You can start small by looking into high dividend yielding stocks. Quality blue chip companies pay as much as five to ten percent dividends per year, on a quarterly basis, simply for owning their shares. This means that for every extra thousand dollars that you manage to save and invest, you can count on another fifty to one hundred dollars coming in per year. On top of this, there is the possibility for capital appreciation in the value of the stock's shares.

There are many other ideas out there for generating additional passive investment income. You should take the time to read about them. This way you can learn what method works best for you to bring in extra monthly or quarterly income.

How The Rich Use Leverage to Achieve And Secure Wealth

There are countless books out there that you can read by self proclaimed or so called financial gurus. Some of them are helpful to you, while others are less useful.

One book that will teach you some concepts that you have probably not heard anywhere else before is called "The Wealthy Code" written by George Antone.

About the Author George Antone

It is useful for you to understand something about the background of the author and why he speaks on this subject as an authority. George Antone proves to be a financier, investor, entrepreneur, long time real estate investor, and best selling author. He has years of experience with both commercial and residential types of property investing.

Besides this, George is a managing partner in a venture capital company called Full Throttle Ventures. Their successful start ups include a media finance firm, a finance firm for renewable energy, and a distressed residential properties financing outfit, among others.

As a nationally known and veteran seminar speaker, George has taught many thousands of individuals around the United States about his successful ideas. Through his teachings, these people have learned to improve their lives as a result of their newly gained financial understanding. George's students are quick to attribute the secrets of their successes to his critical concepts and teachings.

The Code That The Rich Employ

George Antone's latest book is actually about how an incredibly wealthy individual decided to share his imminently practical concepts for growing wealthy with the author. In the book, you see the code that the rich employ. Antone reveals the powerful minutia surrounding this code within the pages of the work.

This permits readers of the book to comprehend the critical concepts that they need to understand what wealth is, how to accumulate it, and finally the ways to become a rich person themselves. The book is touted as a basic and easy for anyone to grasp work on the subject. It may be difficult for complete beginners to fully appreciate. Certainly, it does take readers through extremely potent and advanced ideas that will enable you to grow rich.

The Wealthy Code on Passive Income

Passive income is a major component topic of the book "The Wealthy Code." George Antone shows you the reader how this is among the greatest weapons of the wealthy that they utilize to become and to stay rich. If you are not familiar with passive income, this is a concept that you have to learn to understand and use for yourself.

Passive income is money that comes from an activity that you are not actively involved with on an ongoing basis. The classic example of it is real estate rental properties, although there are various other kinds as well. Stock investments that pay dividends and bond investments that pay coupon interest payments are other examples of the concept. Limited partnership businesses that you do not actively participate in are another type of passive income investments.

You are probably like many people who are very excited by the concept of passive income investments, but you simply do not have the confidence and understanding of the way to proceed with this type of investment that produces income. Many different gurus speak and write about which of these different kinds of investments that produce passive income are the best ones for you to pursue. They all have their benefits and downsides to them, and every guru has his or her favorite type of passive income investment.

"The Wealthy Code" is different in that it does not tell you which of these types of investments that you need to chase. Instead, it teaches you precisely what you have to understand about amassing wealth through this means of investing. George Antone goes through all of the important secrets that the rich understand on how to produce passive income. The author then leaves it up to you to decide which of the various means that you can actually do this with is best for your personal scenario and investment style. His ideas work for all of them.

The Wealthy Code on Risk Mitigation

"The Wealthy Code" does not simply go into the types of investments that you have to work with in order to get ahead financially. It also covers the concept of risk mitigation. George Antone walks you through the particular elements that you have to be alert for and mindful of, such as the types of risk that are present.

Every investment comes with some type of risk. This might be risks to your capital directly, risks that your return will be lower than the rate of inflation, or risk that you missing a better opportunity when you tie up your money in an investment with low yields.

The author teaches you how to understand and evaluate risk, so that you are not afraid of it, but are instead comfortable with it. He then takes this the critical step further to show you the practical ways that you can lower the risks associated with any and all investments. Once George Antone demonstrates to you the effective means to reduce your risk with your passive income investments, he then goes on to show you the way that you are able to effectually build up wealth while you use these risk mitigation strategies.

The Wealthy Code on Leverage

"The Wealthy Code" has a lot to teach you about leverage. It is unlike other works on the subject that are one hundred percent in favor of it all of the time. Author George Antone understands that leverage is a two edged sword that you must wield very carefully. He explains the dangers of it to you so that you are well aware of what you are getting into when you take out a loan for any type of investment purpose.

He gives cases of good and bad uses for leverage. Where other authors talk up good and bad debts, "The Wealthy Code" shuns this traditional concept in favor of you understanding the powerful concept of leverage and how you can use it properly and safely. These ideas are more potent as they are relevant to all types of financial transactions.

Final Verdict on The Wealthy Code

"The Wealthy Code" has a world of insight to offer you on the ways and means that the rich use to achieve and secure their wealth. The author goes through how to steps to apply these secrets to the actual real world too. In this way, George Antone is picking up where other writers leave off on practical steps for you to apply this critical knowledge.

The valid criticism leveled against the book has to do with the ease of understanding it. For a reader with an intermediate or expert knowledge base on finance and investing, this book can be finished quickly. True beginners will have a difficult time with it. Because of this, a person who is new to investing should probably start with an easier book and work up to this one. With this in mind, the author recommends that you read "Rich Dad - Poor Dad" by Robert Kiyosaki.

Why Is Net Worth A Meaningless Number in Practice?

Calculating your net worth is an activity that many financial advisers strongly recommend that you do from time to time. It has gained such acceptance as a gold standard measurement within the financial planning community that it is almost never challenged anymore.

The truth is that while figuring up your net worth is recommended all of the time, it does not provide you with a value that has any meaning in making your financial plans. The subsequent paragraphs go through the ins and outs of net worth calculations and why there are better calculations that you should perform in your own financial planning.

What Is Net Worth?

You should first understand what the definition of net worth is to better understand the concept. Net worth proves to be the difference between what your assets are and how much that you owe in debts. It can be figured up for you personally, for a business, or for another organization. When you figure up your net worth, you should work with all of your assets in the equation.

Assets are comprised of cash that you have, real estate, major assets like cars, stocks, and additional investments.

You are supposed to use the estimates of their current values and not the price that you purchased them for when you prepare this information. The same is true with liabilities that you are collecting for your calculation.

You have to assess these accurately in order to come up with a precise net worth. Liabilities include balances on car payments and mortgages, all outstanding credit card debt that you have, and any balances left on other kinds of loans. Both the total assets and liabilities have to be included and estimated to get an actual net worth picture.

How Do You Calculate Your Net Worth?

Figuring out your net worth is actually not very difficult once you have gathered together all of the information on assets and liabilities. Net worth is simply the difference between what your assets are and the amounts of money that you owe. So calculating up this net worth is simply a matter of adding up all of the assets' values and then subtracting out the total sum of all liabilities and debts. If the value of all of your assets proves to be greater than the sum of all your debts, then you have a positive net worth. If your liabilities' total turns out to be greater than your assets, then you possess a negative net worth.

An Example of Your Net Worth

Looking at an example of your net worth is helpful to understand how to figure it out. If you have thirty thousand dollars in investments and cash, two hundred thousand dollars in real estate, and forty thousand dollars in cars' value, then your total assets are two hundred and seventy thousand dollars.

At the same time, you might have one hundred and eighty thousand dollars in mortgage, thirty thousand dollars in car loans, and ten thousand dollars in credit card bills. This would make your net liabilities two hundred and twenty thousand dollars.

Subtracting your liabilities from your assets will give you your net worth. This means that you would take two hundred and twenty thousand dollars away from two hundred and seventy thousand dollars to come up with a net worth of fifty thousand dollars. One thing to remember when you are figuring up your liabilities is that your mortgage amount owed is not the value of your real estate. This could be more or less than the amount that you owe on it.

Why Do Financial Advisers Recommend That You Figure Out Your Net Worth?

Financial advisers suggest that you figure up your net worth mostly as a means of measuring your financial health. If you could pay off the total of your debt obligations by selling all of your financial assets, then this shows stable and solid financial health. Similarly, if your assets are more than sufficient to cover your debts and obligations, then you are in an even stronger place financially. Understanding your net worth is supposed to help you to keep from overloading on liabilities against your assets. Banks will be less likely to loan you money at competitive rates if they consider you to be a dangerous credit risk.

The second reason that they suggest that you know your net worth is that it gives you a launching point for your financial planning. If it turns out that you do not possess sufficient assets to cover your present debt, then you should avoid making other significant purchases until you liquidate several of your debts.

Because of this, financial planners are in favor of you figuring up your net worth from time to time so that you know where you stand today and where you will probably be tomorrow.

Finally, the financial planners will recommend that you figure up your present net worth to determine what surpluses that you have for investments and savings. Since you do not need the extra money to cover debts, you can afford to tie up the money. They also say that you will possibly discover assets that you were not even aware of that you might commit to investments when you figure up your net worth.

Why Is Net Worth A Meaningless Number in Practice?

All of this calculating of net worth is not inherently wrong. The problem with it is that the measurement gives you numbers that only benefit you in theory. Maybe you have enough assets to cover your liabilities. The reality is that you are not going to sell everything that you have to pay off all of your debts. This would be crazy. What this means is that the net worth number is ultimately meaningless except for as a vague measuring stick.

A case in point is what would happen if you needed money urgently. Maybe you will lose your job and then find yourself in dire financial straights. The net worth value will not tell you anything practical for this situation. You need to know what money that you have readily available. For this scenario, you need an entirely different number that is ultimately more useful.

How Long Can You Live Without Working?

A far better calculation of where you stand financially is also eminently more practical. Instead of spending the time and effort to figure out your net worth all of the time, you should have a solid handle on how long you can live without working. This is the calculation that will tell you where you really stand financially. Net worth assumes that you will always have your job and current rate of pay whatever happens.

The time to live without working calculation will tell you how long your liquid assets can cover your expenses. Should you lose your job or have your pay cut back at work, this is the equation that you need to understand intimately. Ultimately, your financial health comes down to your ability to keep up with all of your monthly obligations should you deprived of this monthly income.

Spend your time figuring out where you really stand in a practical matter like liquid assets versus expenses and not on the theoretical numbers of your net worth. You will be glad that you did.

Why The Poor Want to Own And The Rich Want to Control

You have always heard that there are many important things that separate rich people from poor people. This is certainly the case. Significant differences in attitudes, actions, and practices make a world of differences between the rich and the poor.

One thing that is a distinguishing characteristic between the two groups is their attitude towards possessions and assets. Poor people always want to own things for themselves.

The rich, on the other hand, prefer to control assets rather than to own them outright. In the subsequent paragraphs, you will understand the difference that this makes in real world, practical terms.

What Are the Advantages to Controlling an Asset?

The rich understand that the greatest advantage in their life and investments is obtained when you control an asset rather than own it directly. When you control an asset, you allow the bank or some other financier to own it. They get to have the deed. This means that their money is tied up with it, instead of the rich person's money.

A wealthy person will not care that the bank has the on paper possession of the house, commercial property, hotel, or other producing asset, so long as they get to reap the benefits that the asset produces. If it is a house, they want to live in the mansion. It is not important to them that their money is locked up in it. In fact, they would much rather have their money put to productive uses, like in an investment, than to have it limited to own a house.

If the asset is a commercial property or hotel, the wealthy will want to control the management of the property and gain the benefit of the cash flow and net income that it produces. They will not want the liability and responsibility that comes when they actually own it. They only want to realize the investment returns that the asset produces.

The same is true for producing oil and gas properties and other producing assets. The important factor is the utility, income, and cash flow from the investment. This is what the rich are after, not the pride to be able to claim that they own the property themselves.

Donald Trump As An Example

Look at Donald Trump, who is one of the most visibly successful entrepreneurs and commercial property developers in the United States. His name is branded on countless hotels, casinos, residences, and clubs in Atlantic City, Las Vegas, New York, and Palm Beach. Yet the truth is that he has long ago ceased to own most of these Trump Towers, Trump Casinos, and Trump Plazas.

Donald Trump learned after his first financial empire collapsed that the real secret was to get the banks to be the major owners and partners of the properties, and to simply license his name and manage the various properties.

This way, he still makes the lion's share of the money. Should things go bad, it is not his money that is tied up and committed to the enterprises, it is the various banks' monies.

Now he is wealthier than he was before his massive financial setback, even though he technically owns less. He has become the best known example of this secret that separates the rich from the poor.

What Are the Disadvantages to Owning an Asset or A Property

The poor love to own things. It is probably a result of their feeling like they do not have anything for themselves. When they gain the opportunity to acquire a house or an asset, they are quick to sink all of their money into it so that they can have the pride of ownership. What they do not realize is that they are picking up a number of disadvantages through owning the asset.

The first downside to owning something is that there is opportunity that is lost since the money can not be put to work in another or multiple productive assets that are generating cash flow and opportunities for income. Leverage is this ability to take a small amount of money and to control a far greater amount in assets than the actual money committed to the asset will literally secure. Poor people miss the point of this critical concept completely. In their desperate need to own things, they simply lose out on the opportunity to control and use assets.

Another downside to you owning an asset or property is that you must pay for the property taxes on an asset when you actually own it. Rather than give banks this responsibility and onerous expense like rich people do, poor people cling to it as a badge of honor.

Rich people know that it is better to save their money and use it for more productive purposes. This is one reason why the rich pay a far smaller amount of money in taxes as a percentage of their income than the working poor do.

A final disadvantage that you obtain when you insist that you must own something rather than control it is that you assume the costs and responsibility to keep up the property or asset. Maintenance can be a considerable burden. This is the case with the lessor cost of a house, and it is all the more true with a major corporate office building or large hotel. Once again, the rich would rather let the actual owner of the property have to pay for upkeep and maintenance than to commit their own money to the burdensome expense.

Owning Something Does not Mean That you are Wealthy

Having possession of an asset does not signify that you are wealthy. In many cases, it simply means that you have liabilities that you are confusing with assets. When you own a house, but you are required to make large monthly mortgage payments on it, this creates a negative cash flow every month. Money leaving your account to pay for something constitutes liabilities.

Assets are things that bring in money every month and create positive cash flow for your financial situation. It is exactly this confusion between an asset and a liability that separates the rich from the poor. The rich are far more interested in positive cash flow than they are in actual ownership of something. The poor do not realize that the house that they own causes them to have negative cash flow and drains them every month.

When You Own Something, You Are at Risk of Predators

Predators tend to prey on people who own things. They do not go after people who control them so much. Besides this, people who own assets and houses are the ones who stand to lose if the asset is robbed or stolen. The rich leave all of the liability and risk of physical loss with the owners, the bank. They do not extend their own money and assets to put them at risk so that they lose them to financial predators. This is a painful lesson that the poor only learn after they have become victims.

Now that you understand the differences between the status of owner and controller, you should ask yourself a question. How can you come to control an asset that contributes to your positive monthly cash flow and passive income?

The Six Types of Investors And Their Investment Strategies

When you consider the different kinds of people out there, you will find that not everyone is a great investor. There are some who have not even started to invest, others who are new to the investing trade, and those who are well advanced along the path of successful investor.

You will discover basically six different types of investors in America and the capitalist world. In the subsequent paragraphs, you will figure out what investor level best describes you.

The First Stage of Investor - The Spender

This first stage of investor is really not an investor at all. If you are in this category, you could call yourself a negative saver and investor. Rather than put aside some of your money to invest every month, what you do instead is spend everything that you have. In fact, this is not enough money to support your life style, so you borrow to help continue to shop, purchase expensive cars, buy gorgeous houses, and enjoy nice dinners out.

Spenders are not necessarily people who make low salaries or who have too little income. You who are in this category simply do not have good habits to control, manage, and spend your money. From such bad habits come bad choices and actions.

These give negative results every time. It is critical to advance from this stage to the next one before you find yourself ruined and totally destitute.

The Second Stage of Investor - The Saver

The second stage of investor is the saver. You in this category are also not truly an investor, but at least you are on the right path to become an investor one day. If you are a saver, then you put aside some money each month. You will likely put this money in a low interest savings account, a money market account, a Certificate of Deposit, or a Fixed Deposit.

Many savers put their money aside for future purchases, not investments at all. When you are this kind of saver, you prefer to buy things with cash instead of credit. You believe in working for what you have. Others of you want to have money for a rainy day or for retirement. It is not bad to be a saver, but there is a problem with keeping your money in these kinds of savings vehicles. They pay very poor returns. In today's interest rate environment, the returns can be called negative after you account for tax and inflation rates.

It is good to put savings aside. Many financial professionals will tell you that you need at least six months of savings and better still two years' worth that you can access. This way if your job is eliminated, then you will have some flexibility and time to figure out what to do next. The rest of your money is better off if you put it to work in an investment that might pay an average of eight percent and higher. Savers have to be ready to educate themselves to find high yield and safe investments.

The Third Stage of Investor - Intelligent Investor

The next stage of investor can be called the intelligent investor. When you reach the point to start to study about investments and finance, then you have arrived at this stage. If you are an intelligent investor then you have read the basic books that explain all of the concepts that you need to invest. You will understand about the ways that you can manage your risk properly. You will know all about the wisdom and benefits of diversifying your portfolio.

You will also understand that you can never know too much. Even while you are investing your money to build up your portfolio, you continue to read books, magazine articles, and updates on the various factors that affect your investments. You realize that when you constantly learn more about investing then this will only serve to make you a better investor. This is a good level to find yourself at, but there are higher and better stages of investors that you can become.

The Fourth Stage of Investor - Advanced Investor

Stage four investors are long term investors. If you are an intelligent investor who has learned that you can become wealthy through continuous wise investment, then you have reached this stage of investing. You realize that there is more that you can learn than when you only read and educate yourself. You go to seminars on particular investment products and techniques so that you can better understand them. You have learned advanced concepts such as the power of compound interest.

In this category, you are determinedly chasing your ultimate financial goals towards not only retirement, but also to build up wealth. You keep close track of your expenses. You are very familiar with your assets, liabilities, and debts.

A long term, advanced investor does not waste huge amounts of money on conspicuous consumption. Instead, you put your money to work in investments that will grow and build wealth with time. You have managed to drive away all thoughts of the get rich quick trap and overnight wealth schemes.

The Fifth Stage of Investor - Savvy Investor

In the fifth stage of investing, you are a savvy investor. You have arrived at this level when you do more than simply learn about other people's ideas for good investments. Now you arrange your own investments and deals. Your returns on your investment have climbed to twenty percent and better.

You will likely pursue a wide range of investments that work well for you. You manage risk expertly and stay focused. After you have an investment that is up and running smoothly, you diversify to another investment. You do not become discouraged in economic crises and setbacks. In any type of market, positive or negative, you look for and find opportunities to make money. You control the situation and do not allow circumstances to control you. When you are able to make and forge your own deals, almost like a banker or an investment bank, then you have attained the level of savvy investor.

The Sixth Stage of Investor - Successful Capitalist

The last stage of investor proves to be the successful capitalist. This is the ultimate level that you as an investor can hope to achieve. At this point, you create organizations. You organize other individuals and their time, abilities, and money.

When you create results, or form a successful company, then you are well rewarded for your time and skill. Your returns tend to be around a hundred percent or better.

If you are the person who reaches this level, then you come up with new product ideas and move forward with them. You develop a company and bring on excellent people to market the products. You become a multi millionaire along the way. Your organization will also number other millionaires who assist you in the process.

You know how to use the bank's money and not your own to start up impressive organizations and take advantage of great opportunities. You make your own opportunities through creative thinking and effective strategy. Henry Ford and Thomas Edison were such great successful capitalists in the past. Steve Jobs and Richard Branson are present day examples of them.

So where do you fit in this line up of different investors, and what can you do to move through the different stages now?

ECONOMY

"Managing Resources for Prosperity"

Economy

What If The U.S. Dollar Loses Reserve Currency Status?

If you watch a good amount of financial news or read a number of newspaper or magazine articles, then you have likely already heard the warning bells being sounded concerning the situation of the U.S. government and its increasingly unsustainable debt. What you may not have heard about is the fact that this poses a very real threat to the global supremacy of the American dollar.

This is something that you should think about and protect yourself against, since if other countries choose to no longer accept the American Dollar, or to devalue it to an extreme low, then both your way of life and investments will be severely impacted almost over-night. The subsequent paragraphs explain how this is possible, as well as what the consequences will be if it happens.

Who Is Predicting that the Dollar Will Depreciate?

It may surprise you to learn how many different people predict a substantially lower dollar these days. Best selling authors Robert Wiedemer of "Aftershock" and David Skarica of "The Great Super Cycle" both forecast the housing collapse, financial crisis, and stock market collapse years ahead of them happening. They are calling for a collapse of the dollar.

The country's most successful investor Warren Buffet similarly says the U.S. will inflate away the value of the currency to pay off the astonishing debts and obligations. Bill Gross the managing partner of PIMCO, the world's largest bond fund, says the dollar will fall by at least twenty percent in the next year to two. Legendary currency trader Jim Rogers argues that the dollar is finished, and he is heavily buying gold and silver. This list of respected economists and investors demands your attention to the threat.

What is the Advantage of the U.S. Dollar as the World's Reserve Currency?

So far, the U.S. has been able to get away with massive debts and unsustainable deficits for one simple reason. The U.S. dollar is still the world's reserve currency, as it has been effectively since World War II and literally since the early 1970's.

Because all governments and banks in the world accept and hold U.S. dollars as the comfortable majority of their reserves, the United States is able to simply print more money whenever it can not afford to pay for things that it needs. Besides this, the country can borrow money in its own currency at incredibly low interest rates that you have seen approach almost zero. This benefits you, since your national government is able to provide numerous social services that most other countries simply can not afford.

You personally benefit in another critical way every time that you stop at a gas station. With the U.S. dollar as the reserve currency of the planet, oil and all commodities are all priced in dollars. This causes oil and the by product of gasoline to be incredibly cheap to you as an American.

Just compare how much other members of the richest nations whose currencies are not the reserve currency pay for their gasoline. While the U.S. average price of gas comes in at $2.72 per gallon, in Germany it is $6.82 per gallon, in Great Britain it is $6.60 a gallon, in Italy it is $6.40 every gallon, in France it is $6.04 a gallon, and in Japan it is $5.40 for every gallon.

The United States has become the wealthiest country in the world as a result of the dollar as reserve currency. Imports can all be paid for in dollars. This is only true in the United States. Other countries have to first change their currency into dollars to settle their balance of payments on imports and exports. Interest rates are lower than in most other countries, making loans on houses cheap.

With oil and other commodities cheaply priced in U.S. Dollars, you see an enormous range of inexpensive goods available. Food items and other items that use oil and gas as input are extremely cheap. This makes restaurants and similar outings affordable in America. The level of wealth and excess seen in the United States is simply unprecedented, and most of this results from the benefits of the Dollar as universal reserve currency.

How Does the U.S. Abuse This Reserve Currency Status?

Until the early 1970's, the U.S. was the world's largest creditor. This meant that the country loaned out more money to other countries than any other nation on earth. By the 1980's we had begun to reverse this trend, becoming a debtor nation.

It only took another decade to the 1990's to see the United States evolve into the world's largest debtor.

The transformation has been dramatic, as the amount of debt that the country has taken on in the wake of the financial crisis and economic collapse is over fourteen trillion dollars. The only reason that this has been possible is because other countries continuously loan America money at impossibly low interest rates.

This is not the only way that the country abuses the status of owning the reserve currency. The United States also has printed money electronically since 2007 in increasingly larger amounts.

The shocking truth is that America has more than tripled the amount of dollars in existence in the world in only three to four years. So far, other countries in the grips of the devastating financial crisis have grudgingly accepted this practice, although they have complained loudly over it. The day is coming when they will no longer tolerate it.

What Might Happen to Cause the U.S. to Lose Reserve Currency Status?

A number of things could happen to cause the country to lose its status of reserve currency. The oil producing cartel OPEC might finally make good on its threat to stop pricing oil in dollars. Enough countries might decide to stop treating the Dollar as reserve currency that it finally ceases to be the one.

Another thing that could trigger this devastating event is that the United States might not be able to service the interest on its enormous debt. This is a possibility that you see getting closer by the day, as the country is rapidly closing in on that time.

The Consequences if the U.S. Dollar Loses Reserve Currency Status

There will be dramatic consequences that you can hardly imagine if the Dollar finally ceases to be the reserve currency of the world. Should the dollar be dropped as reserve currency, then the value of the dollar will plummet. The immediate painful effects will be that commodities prices skyrocket. These would no longer be priced in U.S. dollars, and you would see the falling value of the dollar buy fewer and fewer commodities.

Gasoline at five to ten dollars a gallon is not only possible, but highly likely. Along with higher gas prices would come higher prices for anything that is shipped or uses oil and gasoline as inputs. This means practically everything that you buy, from food stuffs and airline tickets, to cars and washing machines, would all cost dramatically more. As prices skyrocket, your lifestyle would sustain a punishing drop overnight.

Unfortunately, this is not the only consequence that you would see of a dollar that is no longer the reserve currency of the world. Interest rates would rise dramatically. They could easily reach ten to fifteen percent. This would wreck housing prices far worse than they are today. It would also cause the stock market to crash and burn by maybe even half in a number of weeks.

As the costs of supplies and materials goes up with the falling currency, businesses would be forced to cut back on employees in the light of their similarly falling sales. Unemployment could reach twenty to thirty percent or more as a result of this. As if this is not bad enough, inflation would be sky high along with the rising prices and disappearing jobs.

You should remember that the only thing that has to occur for all of these terrible things to happen is for other countries to prefer to be paid in anything besides U.S. Dollars. The big question comes down to what will you do to protect yourself and your family in case these events are near at hand?

Time to Make Radical Changes to Your Financial Portfolio

In the last few years since the Financial Crisis and global economic meltdown began, you have probably heard and read a lot of professional opinions from investors, economists, and financial experts who suggest that the economic crisis is not really over, but only moved into a new stage.

The result of all the government interference to save the banking and financial system has been to transfer all or most of the bad debts from the troubled banks to the developed nations' governments themselves.

A new book, "The Global Debt Trap" talks about where this dangerous practice will lead us in the near future. In the subsequent paragraphs, you will see why this work is a must read so that you can understand what will happen next and how you can protect your investments and money from it.

About the Authors

"The Global Debt Trap" is actually written by two well known German Authors Claus Vogt and Roland Leuschel. Claus Vogt proves to be the managing director of Aequitas Capital Partners, a firm that is engaged in asset management. Besides this, he is editor of Money and Markets within the United States, as well as of Safe Money in Germany.

Roland Leuschel is often referred to as the Crash Prophet because of the way that he predicted both the 1980's bull market in stocks and the subsequent horrible stock market crash that occurred in 1987. The co-author is a regular columnist for German's foremost stock market publication, Borse online.

The two writers co-authored a best selling book back in 2004. This is called "Das Greenspan Dossier." This work reads like a prequal to their current "Global Debt Trap." In "Das Greenspan Dossier," Claus Vogt and Roland Leuschel revealed in painstaking details the ways that former Federal Reserve Chairman Alan Greenspan's monetary policies caused a real estate bubble that was unprecedented in American history.

They demonstrated that this bubble was destined to collapse and how it would happen. They also forecast that this real estate bubble collapse would cause a related chain of financial disasters that could not be imagined at the time. This prescient book put the two authors on the map. Its stunning accuracy gives them great credibility. You should pay careful attention to what they have to say in the new book that picks up where the former one left off.

Premise of the The Global Debt Trap

"The Global Debt Trap" begins with an earnest look at how the real estate bubble collapse could be predicted. It then moves into an intense review of how serious the real estate bubble actually was. After these introductory chapters, the book proceeds to explain how the United States' government only made the situation of the devastating real estate bubble so much worse.

Following the utter collapse of this bubble, The American Federal government pushed forward with a dangerous fiscal and monetary policy combination that at its best outcome will only prove to be a potent drug that helps the nation to push off an unavoidable and catastrophic day of financial accounting for these deeds.

In its worst outcome, these actions might instead turn out to be a fatal pill that causes a much greater social and political catastrophe called hyperinflation, or the runaway rise of prices for goods and services in the double and triple digits.

The book points out what a great number of world leaders will admit privately but not publicly. They say that exactly these types of failed government policies and intervention in the capitalist market economy led to the real estate bubble originally. These policies are also pushing the world economy out of one bubble and burst cycle on to the very next one.

What The Global Debt Trap Shows You

Authors Claus Vogt and Roland Leuschel's "The Global Debt Trap" shows you a number of useful and interesting things. They demonstrate the way that the U.S. and developed world economies came to the bad place that they are presently in, how the government leaders let you down, and the ways that they will probably continue to do this.

They argue that the capitalist economic system and freedom of the individual to pursue it are far superior to these interventionist policies of the government. They show you the ways that you can prepare yourself for the future years' effects of the governments involvement in the market economies.

Another insight that is revealing from "The Global Debt Trap" authors is that the so called cure for the financial collapse and debt crisis of 2008 will turn out to be far more severe than the disease itself was. These enormous bailouts on a scale that could not be contemplated in the past will have terrible consequences. The writers show you that this has caused a new crisis of international scope. This is the unsustainable and unmanageable debts of the various developed sovereign nations and governments that took on these debts.

"The Global Debt Trap" reveals to you that as a result of these actions and policies that the Fed encouraged, almost all of the major advanced capitalist economies on the planet are now caught up in the most severe debt trap that you can imagine. They argue that this is the worst debt scenario in the history of the world. The result of this has put your finances, personal health, and even beloved democracy in terrible danger.

To illustrate how serious that this global debt trap really is, the book reviews the fiat money problems that Weimar Germany experienced. They show how this will translate into today's incomparable debt loads that the United States, Japan, and Great Britain have acquired.

The book is forecasting that these governments and others will end up worsening the worldwide economic crisis because of the massive debts that they now hold. They predict that this will cause further international trouble and severe social unrest because of the consequences of these debts on the governments' books.

What The Global Debt Trap Recommends that You Do To Protect Yourself

The authors of "The Global Debt Trap" suggest that you will have to personally manage your investments in the future years. They tell you that this is not a time for you to buy stocks and mutual funds and hold them. They suggest that it is time to make radical changes to your portfolio.

The authors make a great case about how stocks have not historically performed well in times of hyperinflation. They have done better than cash and bonds, but still not well. They give you two rules. You must stay away from terrible losses when the market turns down. More importantly, they state in their second rule that you should look at other investments that will do better in the hyper-inflationary days ahead.

You are warned to steer away from stocks and bonds altogether and consider seriously precious metals like gold and silver, as well as other commodities. Foreign currencies and instruments that perform at an inverse to the markets are also good. The book suggests that you place minimally twenty-five percent of your holdings and money into gold and silver.

Verdict of The Global Debt Trap

This is a book that presents the world's continuing economic problems well and clearly. Besides this, it tells you what you need to do to protect yourself from the future problems. They explain to you the ways that you can use the imminent and most stunning stage of the financial crisis as the means to build up enormous wealth. They tell you that the larger the crisis, the more chances there are to gain for you who plan ahead of the disaster.

What will you do to prepare now yourself for the likely hyperinflation scenario?

Protect Your Money While The US Faces The Financial Abyss

Until recently, unless you were reading deeply and beyond the optimistic economic headlines, you might not have even been aware that the United States' governments finances are in shambles.

In March the fiction began to crack, as well respected economists, think tank groups, and investors alike started to loudly toll the warning bells about the state of the incredible U.S. debt load and unsustainable annual deficits.

Three separate stories have come out just in mid-March that you should be aware of, so that you can know where the U.S. dollar and debt bubbles are headed. This is the only way that you will be able to take measures now while there is still time to adequately protect your money and investments.

Who Says There Is An Imminent Problem with the U.S. Debt and Dollar?

In March, the world's most famous bond investor Bill Gross announced that his fund PIMCO, the largest such bond trading fund in the world, had sold off all of its considerable U.S. government debt. This fund manages $237 billion and is widely followed throughout the world. Gross stated that he foresees a major financial crisis that threatens to seriously erode all Americans' wealth.

He fears that the Federal Reserve is playing a dangerous game with money printing and inflation and is ignoring the peril of the unfolding scenario.

He is not alone in his worries for the status of the nation's finances. Legendary billionaire investor Carl Icahn is so fearful of a stock market crash that he has cashed out a great amount of his ten plus billion dollars and has closed up his investment fund operations. To this effect, he has given back nearly two billion dollars to his investors rather than risk their money in the midst of the worrisome economic scenario and ongoing troubles in the Middle East.

Both of these widely respected investors are offering you an important warning. If it were only them sounding off about the state of fiscal economics in the United States, you might simply shrug your shoulders and say that the smart money was simply wrong this time. After all, isn't that what the talking heads on the financial channels and the politicians in Washington keep preaching, that everything is fine and the worst is behind us?

Economists, Think Tank Groups, and Reports are Warning About the Federal Debt and Money Printing

A prominent member of Ben Bernake's own Federal Reserve board is the lone voice crying out from the stimulus happy Fed about the dangers of the runaway printing press to the future of the U.S. The Federal Reserve Bank President for Dallas, Richard Fisher, stated the last week of March that the American debt and fiscal situation has reached the tipping point.

He has begged the Federal Reserve to not engage in any additional stimulus activities.

Fisher told the University of Frankfurt that the U.S. will soon become insolvent, if it keeps walking on the road that the fiscal monetary authorities have set it. The only question is how soon.

A new report released in mid March that spelled out a similar theme as Richard Fisher is equally ominous for the future finances of the U.S. The Sovereign Fiscal Responsibility Index ranked thirty-four different nations by their capabilities of handling their financial challenges. You may think that the U.S. at least placed in the top half of the results. In fact, it came in at 28th out of 34th.

Just behind the U.S. were such insolvent and bailed out nations as Ireland and Greece. Meanwhile, Australia, New Zealand, Estonia, Sweden, China, and Luxembourg make up the top of the list. This report is imminently credible as it is put out by an organization headed by the former U.S. Comptroller-General David Walker.

It is a dire commentary on the sustainability of the American financing and debt system. If the government does not take dramatic spending cut actions and raise taxes immediately, then Walker predicts that the U.S. will face its own devastating debt crisis over the coming two or three years.

What Are President Obama's People Saying About the U.S. Debt and Economic Situation?

As if the former comptroller general of the U.S. and Fed Reserve Dallas President's warnings are not sufficient to alarm you, there are even people directly appointed by the present spend thrifty administration that are saying much the same things. The President's Council of Economic Advisers' members have come together to release their own report on the subject of America's rapidly rising indebtedness.

Ten of them, who represent both Republican and Democrat chair members of the council, have written an open letter that Politico has published recently. It states that America's shocking budget deficit has become so large and dangerous that is may cause a crisis that literally dwarfs the 2008 financial meltdown. They state that in order to save the country from its overwhelming financial mess, the government will have to cut spending dramatically.

These panel members write that Erskine Bowles and Alan Simpson, the budget watchdogs who headed up the Deficit Reduction Commission of 2010, have suggested that this Federal deficit will soon become a severe threat to the American economy. With the 2011 budget deficit projected at over $1.5 trillion dollars, this marks the third year in a row that the deficit has exceeded a trillion dollars per year. This year will set a new record for level of American budget deficit.

Even though these panel members who wrote the letter do not agree on specific steps to address the critical issues, they do concur that the federal budget deficit is a serious threat to the nation that demands immediate attention. They warn that America's lenders will soon lose patience with the nation's spending spree. When this happens, the bond markets will turn their attacks on the U.S. This will cause a crisis that is far greater in size, scope, and devastation than was the one in 2008, they warn.

The panel and the Bowles-Simpson report both argue the same thing. The federal government will have to take a hatchet to discretionary spending as soon as possible or face financial collapse. Both Bowles and Simpson have warned that the United States will struggle against a ruinous fiscal crisis in two years or less if this spending is not reigned in quickly. Simpson has stated that he believes this crisis will hit in under two years.

Unfortunately, Republicans and Democrats in Congress are currently fighting over whether there should be $30 billion or $60 billion in cuts when half a trillion or more are urgently needed.

Save Your Money and Investments Before the Government Is Officially Insolvent

Reasonable people can no longer dismiss the very real possibility that the U.S. government will lose control of its wild spending and money printing experiment begun a few years ago. With this in mind, you have to wonder what you should do to protect your money and investments from the crisis that well respected national economists, think tanks, and investors are saying is but a year to two away. There are a few places that you could put your money to work so that it actually gains in value as the dollar crashes with U.S. government debt.

The most obvious places are gold and silver. You may fear that you have come along too late to get in on the monumental rise in gold that has already risen over six fold in the last ten years. Silver presents another opportunity. It is called the new gold. It has not yet even risen close to its early 1980's high of $68 per ounce. At current levels, it would have to almost double in price to just achieve those levels. The inflation adjusted high for silver is in fact more than $150 per ounce in today's severely devalued dollars.

For more details on silver investment opportunities take a look at my new book Building Wealth with Silver.

When the smart money and economic advisers have both come to an agreement on the near future of the U.S. government fiscal position, it is time for you to ask yourself a hard question.

Should you ignore the proverbial writing on the wall that a dangerous economic catastrophe is fast drawing nearer at a time when those who have studied the matter intimately and have much to lose are cashing out and moving to protect their investments?

<u>POLITICS</u>

"Banking and Government Interventions"

Politics

How To Prepare For Significantly Greater Inflation Levels?

If you have turned on the financial news lately, then you will have probably seen an analyst or economist on the screen who tells you about the possibility that the dollar will significantly lose its value and that inflation will seize hold of the U.S. economy.

You might dismiss this as an extremist point of view, but it continues to grow in acceptance and influence. A number of books have been written about the potential for a U.S. dollar collapse in the last one to three years.

One of the more interesting of these warning books is "The Dollar Meltdown" by Charles Goyette. Charles Goyette presents a point of view that you should at least seriously consider as you busily accept the official line that the economy is recovering and everything is fine in the United States.

About the Author Charles Goyette

The author of the "The Dollar Meltdown" Charles Goyette is a libertarian radio show host with an impressive following. He is an expert on the precious metals gold and silver. He has achieved the status of New York Times best selling author along the way.

How is The Dollar Meltdown Laid Out?

"The Dollar Meltdown" is comprised of four sections. It breaks down into where the American dollar and economy are presently, the history of how the economy and currency reached this point, the events that will probably occur in the near to medium future, and the ways that you can safeguard your money from the dollar cataclysmic events that are imminent.

Along the way, the work provides you with a good explanation of a number of different finance and economic topics. Among these are the rising national debt, the government bailouts, the Federal Reserve and their reckless monetary policy, the threat and dangers of inflation, and the part that gold plays in the value of currency all through history.

What is the Premise of the Dollar Meltdown?

Charles Goyette provides an easy to understand premise in this work with an ominous title. He claims that the incredible and unparalleled national debt of the United States that is now combined with constant interference by government authorities are steering the nation into ruin. This will lead to significantly greater inflation levels and the devaluing of the American dollar.

You should be prepared for the fact that this is not a painless introduction to the fall of the U.S. dollar. Economists who are followers of the Austrian school of economics will wholeheartedly agree with Goyette's ideas. As a refreshing change from many works on the topic, the book does not protect or defend either Republicans or Democrats. Instead, it labels them all as financial manipulators and resource spend thrifts.

How Will Inflation and Dollar Devaluation Come About As A Result?

Because of all of the rash intervention on the part of the federal government, the United States is headed straight into the uncharted waters of uncontrollable inflation. The author points out some grim statistics. In only the short span of time from the peak of the financial crisis in September 2008 through March 2009, the Treasury and Federal Reserve increased the dollar money base by two hundred percent.

With additional quantitative easing programs part one and part two since then, it is now up over three hundred percent. This will lead to an over supply and cause too many dollars to be chasing too few goods. When that happens, the prices of goods and services will increase dramatically. If you have followed the prices of gold, oil, and food stuffs lately, you know that this has already begun to happen in earnest.

The higher number of dollars in existence is not the only threat that will cause inflation. The national debt situation is a second nail in the economic coffin. As the debt topped fourteen trillion dollars, a greater number of foreign holders of dollars have begun to complain and to worry about the future value of their dollar positions.

When these foreign governments and investors start dumping their dollars, not only will the value of the dollar begin to drop precipitously, but still more inflation will occur. If you think this series of events is unlikely to actually happen here, then consider that a number of countries are already beginning to change out their dollar reserves to Euros and gold right now.

Why Is The Government Not Nervous About Their Dangerous Game?

Goyette explains why the government so rashly continues to pursue this dangerous game with the country's currency and potential inflation. It is because they have always relied on inflation in order to further their economic aims. Mild inflation serves their purposes in making the national debt look like they can manage it.

Helicopter Ben Bernake, Federal Reserve chairman, has been a master manipulator when he claimed that deflation is the real danger all the while he increases the supply of dollars in the world dramatically. Since the government is the nation's largest debtor by far, they stand to gain the most from higher inflation on a manageable level. With four percent inflation, the fourteen trillion dollar debt depreciates by five hundred and sixty billion dollars each year.

Goyette spends a good amount of time arguing that the government is not really capable of staying a step in front of the national economy. Their inflationary policies will not help out the economy at all. He states at one point that when you believe that a little inflation is good it is equivalent to the argument that a couple of termites are useful.

What Advice Does the Dollar Meltdown Offer You?

Because of these pending problems, Goyette offers you some practical advice for how you can save your money from runaway inflation. He says that you should start by putting a quarter of your money into silver and gold that you actually hold physically. The book provides you with excellent practical advice on the ways and places from which you should obtain it.

The chapter that tells you to buy gold is probably the most helpful one in the work. This is where his knowledge of precious metals is best displayed.

The author also spends several chapters in this last section on how to protect yourself and your money and other ways that you can appropriately invest. He has a chapter on silver. He also has ones that follow on how you can prudently and practically invest in oil, other natural resources, commodities, bonds in an inverse strategy, and currencies of other countries. You should read these with an open mind, and keep in mind that this is solid, useful advice.

What is the Verdict on the Dollar Meltdown?

"The Dollar Meltdown" offers a point of view that is gaining in following. It is worth reading even if you do not agree with it, simply so that you can have a better rounded perspective on the economic situation in America today. The format of the book makes it entertaining. It is full of sobering facts and interesting and well informed anecdotes.

You may not agree with the author's conviction that the government is using its economic policies to transform the nation into a communist like central command economy. But you will have a hard time arguing with his cut and dry statistics that cover inflation and currency devaluation.

If he and the various other authors who make a similar case are right about the upcoming American economic picture, then the advice that this book offers you could save the future value of your money and investments.

Why Would The American Government Engage in Austerity?

The news has been full of upsetting and frightening pictures of rioting and protesting that you have witnessed throughout Europe in the last year. They started in Greece and quickly spread to larger economies and countries such as Spain, Italy, France, and even Germany and Great Britain.

Most of these violent protests have been caused by these countries implementing austerity measures. Austerity is a word that you may be unfamiliar with like most Americans. Yet it is one that you should learn the definition of, since austerity is no longer a scenario that is confined to debt laden nations in the European Union. The sobering truth is that austerity has already landed in America, whether you are aware of it or not.

What Exactly Does Austerity Mean?

Austerity is a word that has become more important and prevalent in recent years. It has taken the spotlight to the point that Merriam-Webster named it the official word of the year for 2010. Despite this fact, austerity is a concept that is still vague to the majority of Americans.

Austerity refers to a government policy that involves cutting back on spending. This is done in an effort to reduce an imbalance in public revenues versus expenditures. It is often forced by a drop in government revenues or economic decline. The end result that affects you personally is that austerity leads to a reduction in public services, spending, and benefits. Austerity often leads to unpopular increases in taxes as well.

Why Would A Government Choose to Engage in Austerity?

The fact remains that no government willingly chooses to enter into a policy of austerity. It is usually forced on them by the circumstances of a harsh economic reality. When the government is no longer able to pay for its expenses with current income, and it can no longer borrow to cover the shortfall, then it has no choice but to cut back on spending or to raise taxes.

Usually they resort to both of these means to fix the problems. This explains the scenes of discontent that you have witnessed on the evening news that have plagued both the wealthy and poorer nations of Europe alike.

How Can Austerity Have Come to America?

So far, the U.S. Federal government remains the only major Western country to not accept the economic reality and to engage in austerity practices. While the more realistic and responsible European governments have admitted that it is necessary to cut back on the deficits and to reduce the debts that they wracked up during the financial crisis of 2008 to date, the U.S.

Federal government continues to insist that it can spend significantly larger amounts of money than it brings in through taxes.

The national deficits for 2010 and 2011 both substantially exceeded a trillion dollars. Yet even though the national public debt is now over fourteen trillion dollars and hovering around one hundred percent of annual GDP, the Federal government continues to practice its policies of runaway spending.

Though you have not yet seen austerity be officially forced on the American government at the national level, it has already begun to happen on a state and local level. When you consider that fully forty-eight of the fifty states in the union are officially broke, you begin to see the problem. Since the states are not permitted to run their budgets and finances in deficits, austerity has been forced on them by falling tax bases and rising costs for unemployment benefits.

It is not only the states that are in serious financial trouble, but also the municipal local governments. As property taxes have continued to drop to lower levels along with home prices that continue to fall and show no real signs of rebounding any time soon, the primary source of income for cities and counties has been cut back severely. This has forced them to rethink their spending habits on a large scale too.

What Are the Effects of Austerity throughout America So Far?

Even though there has not been official austerity on the national level to this point, the increased debt to GDP ratio is beginning to have an effect on your standard of living. The economic growth rate of countries with high debt levels is lower as a result of the drag created by large interest payments on that debt.

Two economists Carmen Reinhart and Kenneth Rogoff have determined that nations that have public debts that are greater than ninety percent of their GDP will have an economic growth that averages 1.3 percentage points less each year than countries that possess a lower debt level. With the United States having just surpassed this all important benchmark, a return to the higher growth rates of the past looks less likely all the time.

Real and tangible effects of austerity on you and other Americans is evident in a number of ways on state and local levels. Since states and local governments can not borrow to continue their spending, they are making painful cutbacks. Some of these include cuts to public education, to public services like police and fire, and to badly needed public infrastructure projects such as bridge and road repairs and improvements.

Libraries have to close earlier, fewer teachers are employed by public schools to teach your children, and response times from emergency services are longer. This is only the beginning of the effects of austerity. Some states are taking them a step further and following in the European nations' footsteps of cutting back on public employee salaries and retirement benefits. Others are accelerating layoffs. This only increases the magnitude of the problem, as laid off employees become eligible for state coffers' paid unemployment benefits.

How Does Individual Level Austerity Affect the U.S.?

You have also probably witnessed the affects of austerity already in your own private individual or family spending habits. How many of you still go out to dinner at the same frequency that you did before the financial crisis of 2008 began? When was the last time that you upgraded your house or cars?

The national statistics show that Americans have been delaying large ticket item purchases for several years now.

This helps to explain why home prices do not rebound. Banks will not make loans at the same lax standards as they did in the past, and on top of that, people like you are deciding to avoid any risky move that might expose them financially in a still very much financially uncertain time. As you spend less money and save more, this serves to do more than simply lower your own lifestyle.

The reduced spending combines to drag on any hoped for economic recovery. Businesses see the still gyrating consumer confidence and spending numbers and refuse to increase their new hires. This helps to explain why the official unemployment rate is still right about nine percent, only a percent below its multiple year high, four years after the financial crisis and Great Recession began.

It is easy to see how the effects of personal austerity are impacting the national economic picture as a whole. For things to get significantly better economically, a larger number of consumers will have to shake off their doubt, uncertainty, and personal austerity habits. The question is who wants to be the first to step out on that limb in these difficult and unsure economic days in which we live?

Will Precious Metal Prices Rise With a New Gold Standard?

Any of you who have watched the astronomic rise in gold and silver prices over the last decade know that the dollar is rapidly losing value. It is not only consistently decreasing in worth against the precious metals, but also against most major currencies. The Euro has risen more than forty percent against the dollar since its introduction at the end of the 1990's.

A more shocking comparison is that the Dollar is only worth around thirty-five percent of it's mid 1990's value against the Swiss Franc today. Many people have looked for an answer to the long term decline underway in the dollar. Fortunately, a solution does exist. If we go back on the gold standard that the U.S. government abolished in 1971, then the forty year American currency decline can be halted and even reversed.

What Is the Gold Standard and What Are Its Advantages?

The gold standard refers to a direct link between the quantity and worth of a nation's money and the total gold that it owns. Since the paper currency is backed up by a fixed quantity of gold, individuals who have the nation's money are able to give it to the government in exchange for the pre-determined amount of gold from that country's physical reserves.

For most of the history of the United States and modern Great Britain, the majority of Western countries of the world operated on the gold standard. During those periods, the values of currencies against one another proved to be extremely stable.

This first benefit of the gold standard is that a country's money is guaranteed by an actual hard asset. As the currency is stable, the economy gains the advantages of stability and better self regulation. The government is only allowed to print up so much money as it possesses in physical gold.

The second benefit of this lies in tame inflation. When the money is limited by the amount of gold that a country has, there is little problem with too much money in existence to chase too few goods. This also keeps governments from running up debts and annual deficits, since these are not able to be greater than the country's gold reserves.

Finally, the gold standard provides rewards to countries that are more productive. Those nations that export a greater amount of goods, like Germany and Japan, will build up greater reserves of gold. This allows them to print up additional money that they can plow into their businesses as additional investment. Nations who run trade deficits are penalized under the gold standard, as they are forced to hand over their gold to creditors in order to make up for the trade imbalances.

Could the U.S. Return to the Gold Standard?

The United States actually has history to draw on for a return to the gold standard. During the Civil War, the country left the gold standard in order to print up more money to pay for the conflict.

Gold prices catapulted from twenty dollars to a few hundred dollars. In the 1870's, congress enacted the Resumption Act.

This allowed for a return to the gold standard over a three year transition period. In the meantime, the country had to stop printing dollars and withdraw some bills from the financial system. They were forced to balance the national budget. At the end of the three year period, the dollar returned to its formerly stable value that continued on more or less un-interrupted until the country abandoned the gold standard again a century later.

For the country to return to the gold standard, there would definitely need to be a transition period of several years. Otherwise, there would be a bumpy conversion period back to the gold standard. Proponents of the gold standard, like Ron Paul, have suggested that there could be a few years where there were gold backed bills competing against paper only bills. Within a few short years, gold would crush the paper alternative.

How Soon Could the U.S. Go Back to the Gold Standard?

History gives us clear guidance on how soon the U.S. will choose to go back to the gold standard for its currency. In the history of paper money, there has never been a currency that made it longer than forty-two years from the point that its physical backing has been dropped. Since President Nixon abandoned the gold standard in 1971, this means that the country should back its currency up with something tangible again by 2013. And it will be about time, too.

Consider how rocky the economic picture has been for the United States in the forty years since the country did away with the gold standard.

The American economy has endured three oil price shocks that were caused by the dollar, suffered from in excess of three recessions, and watched the capital base contract as the dollar has decreased by over 95% in purchasing power as measured against gold and silver. This is all the result of using a unit of exchange that has crashed and burned in value in the ensuing forty years.

What Will The Effects of Going Back to Gold Standard Be?

There will be a number of effects of backing the dollar up with gold again. On the downside, the government will lose much of its ability to control the national economy. This is because the Federal Reserve will not be capable of manipulating the money supply to raise interest rates to fight inflation or to drop the same rates during a recession. Economic growth will be based on trade surpluses and higher gold reserves.

The flip side to this is that the American money supply will stay constant. A balanced budget will be mandatory. Fiscal discipline will be forced on a government that will be limited in its ability to intervene in the economy. This is the reason that many people so strongly want to return to the stability of the gold standard.

Gold prices would stabilize and stay in a narrow trading range once this happened as well. At present, gold and silver prices reflect the instability of the paper only currency that we use. Once the transition to the gold standard is complete, gold will no longer have wild gyrations that are so common today.

Before the transition was completed though, you would likely be looking at significantly higher gold prices.

This is because the obligations of the U.S. government today stand at fourteen trillion dollars, while the U.S. gold reserves of 8,133.5 tons valued at $1,400 per ounce are only worth just over $366 billion dollars. You see that this gross mismatch would require gold prices at four times higher than they are now, or around $5,500 per ounce, for the nation to honor all dollar claims with gold.

Another effect when the U.S returns to the gold standard is that the rest of the world will have to follow suit. Countries that do not will watch their currencies plummet in value as investors flee to those that are as good as gold.

After all, which currency would you rather own - one that is guaranteed by the metal most valued in all of human history, or one that asks you to rely on only the full faith and credit of the government that issued it?

Politics

<u>MONEY</u>

"Understanding the Medium of Exchange"

Moving Forward With The Monetary Paradigm Transition

Zeitgeist: Moving Forward, by director Peter Joseph, is a feature length documentary work which will present a case for a needed transition out of the current socioeconomic monetary paradigm which governs the entire world society.

This subject matter will transcend the issues of cultural relativism and traditional ideology and move to relate the core, empirical "life ground" attributes of human and social survival, extrapolating those immutable natural laws into a new sustainable social paradigm called a "Resource-Based Economy".

This film will feature experts in the fields of public health, anthropology, neurobiology, economics, energy, technology, social science and other relevant subjects which relate to social operation and culture. The three central themes of the work are Human Behavior, Monetary Economics, and Applied Science.

Put together the work creates a model of understanding the current social paradigm; why it is critical to move out of it - coupled with a new, radical, yet practical social approach based on advanced understandings which would resolve the current social woes facing the world today.

One of the unique attributes of this work, which separates it in style from most documentaries, is that it has a parallel dramatic/cinematic theme, with notable actors, which abstractly plays out various gestures related to the overall message of the film. The work also vigorously employs numerous 2d and 3d visual abstracts/animations, while returning to the standard, traditional documentary orientation as the foundation.

Release Date

Zeitgeist: Moving Forward is to be released in 60+ countries and in 20+ languages starting January 15th 2011. This large scale release is not associated with any major distributor. Part of the counter-culture expression of this approach is to bypass all corporate media involvement and utilize independent groups, in a non-profit manner, which will show the work in their respective regions.

Most of these groups are in affiliation with various activist communities, including "The Zeitgeist Movement", which is a sustainability advocacy group seeking a social transition into a new socio-economic paradigm, away from the growing distortion of the monetary system and its consequences.

Zeitgeist: Moving Forward is a non-commercial project, which means it will be available for free acquisition via internet in both online viewing form and full DVD download.

ZeitgeistMovingForward.com will also have a physical $5.00 DVD available in mid to late January.

The Global Theatrical Premiere will be presented by The Artivist Film Festival organization on January 15th 2011 in Los Angeles, CA

About the Director

The director, producer, writer, cinematographer, composer, editor and narrator of the work, Peter Joseph, was inadvertently brought into recognition within the documentary film community with his award winning, controversial, 2007 work "Zeitgeist: The Movie" which obtained over 100,000,000 views online during the first year of its publication. This film was not a film at all in its original conception, but become one after it achieved global acclaim.

In 2008, a sequel to the work, entitled "Zeitgeist: Addendum", was premiered at the Artivist Film Festival in Hollywood CA. As with its predecessor, the award winning "Addendum" was a huge viral internet phenomenon obtaining over 50,000,000 views within its first year.

After the release of this sequel, Joseph then founded a social movement inspired by the public reaction - called "The Zeitgeist Movement". This global organization, with now over half a million subscribers across 200 countries, works to begin a transition of culture into a new sustainable economic paradigm and Zeitgeist: Moving Forward is, in part, a media expression of the same focus. "The Zeitgeist Movement" is an extension of "The Venus Project"- an organization established by industrial designer - Jacque Fresco - which is also featured in the film.

"Zeitgeist: Moving Forward" is the third installment in what has now become a cultural film series project which continues to consider the current "Zeitgeist" - which means "The Spirit or Awareness of the Time" or culture.

For more information about Zeitgeist: Moving Forward, including release dates: www.zeitgeistmovingforward.com

The Three Types of Income And Their Tax Scenarios

You should know that all money that you bring in is not equal. This is to say that there are three different types of income that the Internal Revenue Service defines.

These are earned income, portfolio income, and passive income. Each of these has their advantages and disadvantages.

Most importantly, all of them are treated differently for income tax purposes. The following paragraphs go through the various types of income and the things that you need to know about their different tax scenarios.

What You Should Know About Earned Income

Earned income is probably the simplest type of income to understand. This is because you like most Americans probably derive the majority of your income from earned income. The definition of earned income is simply all of the wages and income that you make when you work. You make such earned income in one of two ways. You might perform work for a person or company who then pays you. Otherwise, you work in your own business and make earned income as a result of the business operation and transactions.

The Internal Revenue Service includes a number of these types of wages in the category of earned income. This includes tips, salaries, and wages; union benefits paid during a strike; earnings from being self employed; and any long term disability payments that you get before you reach the minimum age to retire.

The advantage to earned income is that you can increase the amount of money that you make through more work. You might pick up additional hours at work and earn overtime pay. You might also pick up a second job to bring in more earned income. If you do well at your job, then you might be given a promotion by your supervisor so that you earn a larger salary, get commissions or bonuses, or make higher wages per hour. Through any of these means, you can increase your earned income. If you work harder and better, then you will be rewarded for it with a greater compensation.

The disadvantage to this form of income is the way that the government treats it for tax purposes. Accountants and wealthy individuals can tell you that the government penalizes money that you make as earned income most severely of the three types of income.

Tax brackets average in the twenty to thirty percent range for this type of earnings. Even money that you put into tax deferred retirement accounts is penalized when you withdraw it, as the Internal Revenue Service treats it as earned income when you take it out for retirement. This is one reason why it is difficult to get ahead and grow wealthy with only earned income. It is a noteworthy observation that even U.S. Senators with their around $175,000 payroll per year do not get rich through earned income.

What You Should Know About Portfolio Income

The second type of income that the Internal Revenue Service defines is portfolio income. This portfolio income is derived from your portfolio of investments. In the world of investments, a portfolio is simply a collection of securities like stocks and bonds, or other investments that comprise an investor's total holdings.

If you plan to cease working for earned income in order to live off of your income from investments, then you are talking about utilizing portfolio income. You can create portfolio income with a variety of different kinds of investments. These could be dividends, royalties, and interest that you make off of your portfolio investments. When you sell an investment, such a stock or real estate, this is called a capital gain. It is also counted as portfolio income.

Mutual funds and stocks pay you dividends in these portfolios. Certificates of Deposit, loans made to private parties, and bonds all pay interest. You earn royalties when you permit another individual or company to utilize a property that you own. You can realize them from your ownership stake in mineral rights, oil and gas wells that produce, and property with timber.

The disadvantage to this type of income is that it is not predictable. An investment portfolio will generally yield a different amount of income every year. This might be more or less than you expect and need. Unlike with earned income, you can not simply put in more time and effort and be assured that you will receive a higher return on your portfolio.

Investments also carry a degree of risk. It is very possible to earn nothing or even to lose principal with an investment portfolio. Risk can be managed and mitigated through wise diversification strategies, but there will always still be risk with portfolio income.

The major advantages to portfolio income are the fact that you do not have to work for it and the tax treatment of investments. With a portfolio, once you have it set up, all that you have to do is to monitor it from time to time. This does not require the enormous continuous time investment that you must put in when you work for someone or run a business.

The tax treatment of investments is also a huge advantage to this portfolio income. Tax rates on dividends and capital gains are significantly lower than for your earned income most of the time. These days, dividends are taxed at either zero percent or fifteen percent. Contrast this with the high tax brackets that most earned income suffers from in the twenty to thirty percent range.

There are also significant tax write offs that the government provides for investments in real estate and oil and gas producing properties. With the right mixture of these assets, it is possible to pay almost no tax on portfolio income, and this is an enormous benefit to it.

What You Should Know About Passive Income

Passive income is defined as income that you generate even though you do not work for it. It is money that you get on a consistent basis, even though you do not have to put in much effort to keep it going. The IRS specifically defines this passive income as business activities where you do not participate materially.

Passive income might be money that you earn from a business that you do not work in, rent that you earn from various properties, money that you earn from advertisements on Internet sites that you own, or royalties from licensing a patent or from publishing a book.

The downsides to passive income lie in the fact that there is often a significant amount of upfront time investment required to set it up. If you will write a book or secure a patent, then you will spend a huge amount of time to accomplish this. Even if you want to establish a website that you can earn advertisement dollars from, this will take you a significant amount of time. In either case, you can also not be guaranteed success.

The upside to passive income is that once you have established it, you can usually count on it to provide you with money for years at a time. This will require little ongoing effort on your part. Yet it can free you up to do whatever you wish to with your time.

Consider this example about the tax advantages of the various types of income. Donald Trump makes millions of dollars per year from his portfolio and passive income investments. Yet he pays a lower percent in tax rates than does his secretary who makes a fraction of his income as earned income. Which tax situation would you rather have?

A New World Order - Two Weeks After The Dollar Crashes

In Mid March, you may have seen the shocking news that the world's largest bond fund, PIMCO, announced that it had completely divested itself of all U.S. Treasury Bonds and bills. This came as a stunning surprise for many investors and analysts. Because this is a major rebuke of the U.S. dollar and American debt, it is something to which you should pay careful attention.

A new book deals with the ramifications that may come from such major votes of zero confidence in the dollar. This is "The Day After the Dollar Crashes" by Damon Vickers. Since it foretells both a drastic change in the American lifestyle and a dramatic future decline in your savings and investments, it should be required reading for both you and all Americans.

The Day After the Dollar Crashes' Author's Biography

Damon Vickers turns out to be the Nine Points Capital Partners' chief investment officer. He has shared investment ideas professionally for twenty-five years. Before the markets tanked in 2000-2003 and 2008, he recommended and took short positions that profited handsomely.

The fund that he capitalized in 2008 made sixty-three percent that year by betting against GM, AIG, Lehman Brothers, and Countrywide, as well as other failed companies of the financial collapse.

Damon Vickers has made appearances on a wide variety of well respected and followed shows around the world.

These include CNBC, Fox Business, Bloomberg, Glenn Beck, CNBC Asia, Japan Public Television, BNN Canada, CBC, and the Today Show. In publications, his writing has been showcased in The Wall Street Journal, The Washington Post, and CNN Money.

Premise of the Day After the Dollar Crashes

Vickers makes a compelling case that the U.S. stands at a dangerous cross roads. Both at home and abroad, Americans live lavishly in a way that is impossible to sustain long term. In his persuasive book about the days after the dollar collapses, Damon lays out the types of circumstances and events that will likely lead to a worldwide financial crash and economic collapse centered on the U.S. dollar's unavoidable fall.

He goes into great details on the occurrences that will probably kick off the malaise, happen in the middle of it, and transpire after a complete collapse. He spends a great amount of time addressing what you as an investor can do to profit in these unsettling times that are coming.

Besides this, Damon's work goes into solutions that the American government could pursue to lessen the blow of the dollar's irreversible decline and future fall. He also explains ways that answers and ideas can be created to address the inexorable new economic forces. He shows you how to make money when you leave behind your old perceptions and take steps to reorder your investments according to the shifting economic reality.

The goal of the work is to remove the fabrications that the media, politicians, and financial experts have artfully created so that investors like you can learn how to take positions that will not only outlast, but outperform, the many holdings that will fail in the financial New World Order.

Strengths of the Day After the Dollar Crashes

Any book that purports to predict the end of the present world financial system had better offer some very hard and irrefutable reasons for why this will occur in the first place. Author Damon Vickers does just this. He lays out an extensive and persuasive group of arguments for why you should take seriously the idea that the most severe financial collapse yet is on the way.

Vickers argues that this catastrophe will make the financial collapse and Great Recession of 2007-2009 look like child's play. For the majority of the book, the author painstakingly goes through the mind numbing amount of debt that the United States has wracked up collectively. It demonstrates time and again through evidence, charts, and analysis that this simply can not be paid back.

Many financial experts and economists have already accepted this argument that the debts can not be repaid in present dollar values. The difference here is how masterfully the premise and arguments are laid out. You simply can not read the book and walk away skeptical of Vickers' evidence and inferences.

A New World Order And a New Currency

What is ground breaking for "The Day After the Dollar Crashes" is the section where Damon Vickers lays out an only two week time frame where the dollar system dies an ignoble death and is replaced by a financial New World Order. This will not happen by accident, but as a result of a premeditated decision by the rising economic power of Asia.

This begins with a Chinese choice to not buy any more U.S. Treasuries. That single day will be the death nail in the dollar's coffin. Over the next two weeks, events will spin out of control in financial markets the world over. Stock market crashes of six to ten percent in a day will become the norm over the following few weeks. Vickers lays out scenes of chaos and rioting, looting of grocery stores, empty ATM machines, and shootings around the world.

Gold will rise as much as three and four hundred dollars a day all the while the dollar is plummeting and other currencies are gyrating wildly around the world. The Swiss Franc will be one currency that holds up and appreciates as others are in tail spins, simply because it is the only paper currency in the world that is still backed up by fixed amounts of gold in bank vaults.

The fact that the events outlined in the book sound more like a movie plot than a realistic prediction of imminent world events is a testament to the compelling nature of the book. It offers enough excitement to be turned into a financial disaster movie. This does not take away from the seriousness of the forecasts. It should not stop you from taking a hard look at the book and the suggestions that if offers you for surviving and thriving in the difficult days that it argues lie ahead for America and the world.

Verdict of The Day After The Dollar Crashes

You may fall in the large group of readers who do not appreciate the author's continued references to an imminent financial New World Order. The truth is that Vickers is not out campaigning for it. He instead suggests that it will come whether you like it or not. As many countries are already clamoring for a replacement to the U.S. dollar, you had best consider the possibilities of this becoming reality and make some real preparations.

A possible downside to the book is the unspecific plan of what you should do to save yourself from the approaching financial tsunami. Damon recommends that you buy gold and silver, but he does not tell you in what form or manner to go about this. Most of his suggestions are concepts and not step by step advice.

The flip side of this is that his advice may be more useful than a literal investment manual, since no one can accurately predict exactly how the crisis will play out. This is ultimately what you will have to ask yourself - would you rather take some precautions that might not be necessary, or instead be unprepared for a potential financial paradigm shift that changes your life permanently?

<u>**TOOLS**</u>

"Instruments for Building a Wealth Foundation"

Tools

The Top 10 Websites To Get Excellent Financial Education

When you are setting out on your quest to achieve your financial goals of investing, building up wealth, and retiring, then you will need to start out by building up a solid personal financial education. You should not feel bad that you find yourself lacking in this important respect, as most people are in the same situation.

Especially the American education system does not teach good financial education at all. You do not have to despair, as there are good means of learning financial education without having to go take college courses or get a degree. In fact, this is even available from the proximity and convenience of your own home and personal computer. I researched for you ten places where you are able to obtain an excellent financial education. The good news is that most of them are available to you for free.

Rich Dad Website

Rich Dad is the investing website home and brain child of Robert Kiyosaki. In case you are not familiar with Mr. Kiyosaki, he is the phenomenally successful real estate and passive income investor from Hawaii.

He has evolved into a best selling author and nationally known speaker as a result of his original multi-million copy selling book "Rich Dad - Poor Dad." The website is rich with information and online articles and mini seminars, but much of it requires a membership for you to participate in it. Still, as pay sites go, it is worth your money and time to join and learn at the feet of a true investing master. You can go to the Rich Dad website at: http://www.richdad.com.

Investopedia Website

The Investing Education Site is more commonly known as Investopedia. Investopedia feature more than just the most complete investing dictionary found anywhere on the Internet. It offers you a great number of both tutorials and articles on almost any topic having to do with investing and finance. This website is helpful to people of all ages and knowledge levels and will benefit equally novices and more seasoned investors. The tutorials are intelligent enough to make the difference between experienced, intermediate, and new investors. This excellent website is found at: Investopedia.com

Professor Wachowicz's Web World

Professor Wachowicz is a University of Tennessee professor. He has assembled an inspiring group of articles and links related to finance for students everywhere. These are arranged by category. Among them are Tools of Financial Analysis and Planning, Introduction to Financial Management, Intermediate and Long Term Financing, and Working Capital Management.

This site does not cover so many investment related topics, but if you are looking to build up your financial issues education, then this is a terrific site at which to spend your time. Go to the website at http://web.utk.edu/~jwachowi/wacho_world.html.

Encyclopedia of Finance

A part of your financial education should be dedicated to the basics of financial information and knowledge. The Encyclopedia of Finance proves to be a tremendous resource for this need. It goes through these important foundational financial concepts in a manner that is simple to grasp and direct. Its greatest asset for you may be the site's Guide to Online Investing, which is a must read before you start doing your own investments. This authoritative site is provided by TDAmeritrade, but it does not require that you open an account to utilize it. The website is located at the following link: http://www.ameritrade.com/education/html/encyclopedia/index.html.

Virtual Finance Library

The Department of Finance at The Ohio State University put together a virtual library of finance. It bills itself as not only suitable for students and professors but also for investors and learners like yourself. This impressive collection of articles and links is offered to everyone at no charge. The Finance Department is currently engaged in updating the various pages to create an even more satisfactory result. This fabulous virtual library is a must read for understanding finance. You can go to the website by navigating to the address http://fisher.osu.edu/fin/overview.htm.

Financial Management Training Center

This Financial Management Training Center is another great free advice and training site on topics having to do with finance and business finance. Matt H. Evans owns and authors it. The most helpful portion of the site for you will be the one that pertains to the short courses. These offer concise and specific knowledge covering a range of particular issues. Among these are budgeting, managing a cash flow, and evaluating financial performance. This site also offers you the convenience of downloading the varying courses in either Word document format or Adobe pdf format. Go the site at http://www.exinfm.com/training/index.html to get started.

Investor Links

At Investor Links, you will discover a tremendous index of financial sites that provide analysis of different industries and company stocks, commentaries on the markets, articles on technical trading, recommendations for the market, and a daily summary of American markets. The site is concentrated around the United States, but it also offers links to international markets. If you are a person who wants to understand the rising world of online investing, then this is a fantastic resource for you to consult. They even have a special section on cyber stocks. Check out this site for yourself by surfing over to http://www.investorlinks.com.

Investor Guide

Part of your goal with your education is to improve your personal finances. A site that will help you to do this and to also boost your ability at investing is Investor Guide, a thorough resource for you.

The great strength of this site lies in its including learning, personal finances, and investment topics. It is extremely well arranged and even includes annotated links to literally thousands of different investment websites. This is definitely worth you spending some time looking through. To do so, simply go to the following web address at http://www.investorguide.com.

Jim Sinclair's MineSet

Jim Sinclair is a legendary precious metals investor, adviser, and former broker dealer. Among his vast experience is his one time role as adviser to the Hunt Brothers in their famous attempt to manipulate and corner the entire silver market. These days, one of his ventures is a subscription and charge free website that he and his colleagues author and operate called JSMineset.

This professional site is his brainchild, and it includes expert reprints of, commentary on, and analysis regarding a wide range of investment and world finance articles from sources all over the world. Especially for you who have an interest in gold and silver as investments, this site is ideal for you. Find Jim Sinclair's wealth of knowledge, experience, and insightful ideas at:
www.jsmineset.com.

Investment Resources for the Independent Adviser

As your knowledge and ability grows, you will find that you require a site to assist you in performing your research on stocks over the Internet. Investment Resources for the Independent Investor is a wonderful choice for this purpose. It offers you a variety of links pointing to precise information that you will find on different investment related websites.

The site is offered by AOL, but is available for free to anyone simply by registering for an account with them. You should use this site or one like it when you are ready to start obtaining high quality research. Log on to the website by navigating your web browser to the following site at: http://members.aol.com/indinvstr/index.html.

Let me know if you know other websites that offer excellent financial education and I will add them here to the list.

WORKING

"Moving Towards Passioned Contribution"

Working

How Many Days Can You Survive Without Working?

When you think about the definition of wealth, there are many out there from which you can choose. A lot of people measure wealth by how much money that they have in the bank. Others consider it to be a function of how large a house that you have or how many expensive and fancy cars that you drive.

A concept of wealth that you may have never before considered is one that measures wealth in time. You have no doubt heard the well worn saying that time is money.

This alternative definition of wealth relates to how much time you can live without having to work. In the following paragraphs, this definition of wealth is considered, as well as what it means for you and the way that you measure your personal wealth.

Wealth As A Measurement of Time

Robert Kiyosaki is the internationally known speaker and writer of the Rich Dad, Poor Dad series. He is the thinker credited with creating this idea of wealth as a measurement of time. By wealth as a measurement of time, he refers to the answer to one simple question. How long are you able to maintain your present lifestyle without having to make any changes to it should you stop working today?

This may sound a little bizarre or even ridiculous at first, but think about what the question is asking you and what the answer will tell you. You might have twenty thousand dollars per month in income and fifteen thousand dollars per month in expenses. This sounds like a lot of income to the casual observer, but if you only have forty-five thousand dollars in readily liquid assets, such as cash, checking accounts, or money market accounts, then you only have the ability to be without work and your income for a mere three months. How wealthy does that make you?

Consider another example. You may only have four thousand dollars a month in income. At the same time, you could have twenty-five hundred dollars a month in expenses. If you have twenty-five thousand dollars in the bank and readily liquid assets, then you possess ten full months of ability to live without being required to work and maintain your lifestyle.

This can be called ten months of wealth time. Which of the two people is better off, the one with the substantially higher income and low amount of savings to expenses coverage, or the one with the significantly lower income but the higher amount of savings to expenses coverage? According to this definition of wealth as time, you who make less money but have a greater savings to expenses coverage are actually wealthier individuals. This is because it is not really how much money that you make that matters. It is how much money that you stay with after your expenses are cleared at the end of the month that defines true wealth.

You are possibly feeling a nervous tightening in the pit of our stomach at this point. This is because the majority of Americans are actually poor in regards to this definition of wealth. How many friends and family members do you know who have enough in readily accessible savings that they can afford to go long without having that bi monthly or weekly paycheck?

The answer is probably an embarrassing few to none. There is no reason to fear though, since there is a simple remedy for this dilemma.

How You Can Increase Your Time Based Wealth?

Now, if you are following this definition and argument of wealth to its logical conclusion, then you are probably wondering how you are able to increase your wealth that is based on this concept of time without work. The answer is so simple that it may surprise you. The key is to find a way to set yourself up so that you can live infinitely long without needing to work. If you could do this in such a way that you were no longer exchanging your time for money, so that your income is greater than the amount of money that you spend, then you would have found the means of achieving unlimited wealth.

The answer to the problem is called passive income. Passive income is money that you generate without needing to perform work in order to earn it. It contrasts sharply with active income that represents money that you earn directly when you provide your time and talents on behalf of an employer or business. If you manage to create a sufficient amount of passive income to completely cover your current expenses and standard of living, then you can be said to have achieved great wealth.

How Do You Build Up Passive Income?

The wealthy do not actually work for money. They make money work for them. If you could figure out how to do this, then you would also become a wealthy person.

That is a good concept, but how do you achieve it in practice? Building up passive income is not as difficult as you might think. There are a number of different ways that you can go about it. Many professional investors like the idea of rental properties. They buy residential properties, such as houses, and rent them out to people.

This creates a monthly income stream that is supposed to be greater than the amount that you make in monthly payments on the house itself. If you were able to put together a little portfolio of rental properties that provided cash flow income greater than your expenses every month, then you would soon reach the point that you achieved true wealth.

Another way to build up passive income is through owning producing oil and gas properties. This sounds like you would have to be a rich person to even get started with it, but the truth is that there are smaller entry level investments in this category. You can very easily become involved with Canadian Oil Trusts for even a few hundred dollars. These securities are sold as stocks on the major American exchanges. They pay out tremendous dividends on the sale of their oil and natural gas every month. Besides this, you gain the ability to realize capital gains on increased share prices when you sell the investments.

You can also build up capital gains through acquiring stocks that pay high dividends. These offer you the same benefit of an income stream on a quarterly basis. Some quality dividend paying stocks offer as much as eight to ten percent returns. Once again, over time the share price can go up, giving you nice capital gains when you sell the passive income producing investments.

Another good way to realize passive income is through starting a business. You can start small businesses in an very affordable fashion over the Internet. E-commerce is getting to be bigger and bigger every day. You might become involved in auctioning goods on eBay as one example. You could create a small web store that grows into a successful cash producing entity as another example.

Stop and ask yourself the question, how many days can you survive without working? If the answer is a disappointing and frightening small number, it is time to do something about it. How will you improve the number of days that you can afford to go without needing to work?

Working

<u>WEALTH</u>

"Pursuing Prosperity with Financial Education"

Wealth

Use Leverage to Boost Your Investment And Increase Wealth

If you have been around the investing world much then you will have heard the term leverage used. The talking heads on the financial channels throw it out all the time.

Leverage is something that you need to understand, since it proves to be the fastest way for you to make money and gain wealth. The subsequent paragraphs teach you about the right kind of leverage and how to manage the risks associated with it.

What Is Leverage?

Leverage is a powerful concept in finance and investing. Leverage is the ability to use borrowed money in order to finance an investment or activity. Companies employ leverage in order to grow their business or expand their product offerings.

You as a private investor can use it to hopefully multiply your gains and not your losses. You utilize leverage any time that you borrow money to finance some type of investment or asset purchase, such as when you take out a mortgage to buy a house.

Types of Leverage

There are several different kinds of leverage that businesses and people can use. Businesses often work with operating leverage that takes into account the amount of fixed assets and costs that they use in operating the business to make profits. Financial leverage has to do with the loans and debt that they take on to earn a greater amount of profits than the costs associated with such debts.

Debt leveraging is the kind of leverage that you will employ as an individual. When you engage in this debt leveraging, you are side stepping the need to tie up all of your money resources when you buy a certain item, such as a house or investments. The goal is to use fewer dollars to boost the profits that you are able to achieve out of the investment. You can obtain this type of leverage by simply taking out a loan at a bank to pay for your asset or investment purchase.

Examples of Leverage

The beauty of leverage is that you are able to control an entire asset using only a small amount of your own money. There are many examples of leverage that will help you to better grasp the importance and power of the concept. Consider the following different real world scenarios with leverage.

Oil Commodity Leverage

Think about a fund or an investor that wants to control a larger amount of the commodity oil. A large hedge fund might put up a half million dollars of cash to control ten million dollars worth of oil. You as an investor might similarly put up a thousand dollars to control twenty thousand dollars worth of the commodity.

In both cases, the principle is the same. The exchange will loan the fund or you the investor the ninety-five percent of the value of the commodity against your five percent investment.

With this twenty to one leverage, you are able to make twenty times the profits that you would be able to achieve without the leverage, as the oil prices increase in value. Leverage is a two edged sword though. If the oil prices drop in value, then your losses will be magnified at twenty times the amount that they would have been without the leverage.

Real Estate Leverage

Real estate is probably the most common form of leverage that most people engage in, even when they are not aware of the fact that they are using such leverage. Most people will put down ten to twenty percent of the price of a house when they buy it. The bank will loan them the other eighty to ninety percent. In the case of an eighty percent loan, the people are actually achieving a five to one leverage.

This means that they gain five times as much with increases in the real estate prices using the leverage as they would with only their own money that they put into the house. If a person buys a $200,000 house with forty thousand dollars down and a hundred and sixty thousand dollar loan, then the person has a five to one leverage because the asset is worth five times as much money as the individual has put down.

Now, if the house increases to $250,000 in value, the person has realized a fifty thousand dollar profit on their original only forty thousand dollar investment.

Without the leverage, the person's gain on the forty thousand dollars invested would only have amounted to eight thousand dollars. You can see how powerful investments that you purchase with leverage can be.

Stocks on Margin Leverage

Many investors also use leverage to purchase stocks and mutual funds. Investment brokerage accounts will commonly allow you to borrow as much as half of the price of a security when you are investing. This means that you are able to acquire two times as much of the investment using the leverage. You achieve a two to one leverage this way. Any gains made when the stock rises will be multiplied by two for you, as will any losses should the stock prices decline.

Risks of Leverage

By now you should begin to understand that there are two sides to leverage. It can make you fantastic returns on your investments when the investments increase in value as you hope. At the same time, it can multiply your losses to shocking levels if they move sharply against you.

Consider this example for the risks of leverage on a small one thousand dollar investment in a stock. If you borrow another thousand dollars to buy two thousand dollars worth of the stock, then you have gained a two to one leverage. If the stock price drops by thirty percent, and the investment falls by six hundred dollars, then you have lost sixty percent of your thousand dollars. You may only realize this loss when you sell, but you will likely be forced to sell as your broker realizes that your investment position is in trouble.

How to Minimize Leverage Risks

There are a few ways to minimize risks with leverage. The most common of these for you as an individual is to only leverage assets that are liquid, or easily salable. This way, if an investment starts to move against you past your tolerance for pain and loss, then you can simply liquidate it and take your hit. At least you stop the bleeding this way.

The other thing that you might do is to negotiate a higher amount of leverage than you actually plan to use. This way, if your investment value is falling, the other party that made you the loan will be less likely to force you to sell your investment at a temporary loss as your part of the investment is significantly reduced. This is commonly done with brokerage accounts, where you may be allowed to buy with two to one leverage, but you are allowed to maintain the position unless it declines to below a three to one leverage point.

How to Calculate Leverage

It is easy to calculate the amount of leverage that you are taking with an investment. Simply divide the purchase price of the investment by the amount of money that you are putting into it. This will give you the leverage as a certain number to one ratio. So a ten thousand dollar investment that you actually put up only a thousand dollars on has a ten to one ratio of leverage.

Building Wealth With Silver - Profit From The Dollar Crisis

If you you are not yet a member of my Wealth Building Course you may not know about my latest book - Building Wealth with Silver. I wrote it last year and it's a direct outcome of the principles I am teaching in my Wealth Building Course. It is now on sale at amazon and Barnes & Noble.

In the following paragraphs you can read a summary of the book. More than the title suggests, this book contains powerful lessons that go far beyond any investment strategy. It provides you with striking clarity on how our money is manipulated by governments and banks.

At the present time - I am guessing - 99% of the public do not have the slightest idea of how money actually comes into existence. The book also covers some profound insights why people are stuck with not having enough money, even though they are doing every-thing they know how to create more of it.

What's Wrong With Money?

While you sleep at night, while you go to work each day, some-thing insidious is actually stealing your financial future. It isn't anyone's fault really. There is a massive reallocation of wealth as we transition into the new economy.

You simply need to find a way to sleep peacefully knowing that your own wealth is safe and secure from those who would take it from you.

Are Your Expenses Eating You Alive?

The middle class is about to be wiped out altogether and only your personal financial intelligence will determine whether you become rich or whether you become poor. There will no longer be that large buffer zone known as the middle class between the rich and the poor. It turns out that how the government mishandles expenses is perhaps the single most important factor in the demise of the middle class.

We are approaching a monetary crisis of epic proportions never before seen.

Since this economic crisis picked up speed in 2008, our government has shunned all sense of fiscal responsibility with:

• Out-of-control stimulus spending
• Record-setting deficits in the trillions
• Job-depleting taxes and regulations

This hits the middle class right where it tends to live most precariously: between earning a living with a good job and paying taxes to support the system. Right under our noses, the bungling Obama Administration and the Federal Reserve continue to create money out of thin air . . . which dramatically erodes the value of everyone's hard-earned dollar.

The Three Major Problems You Are Facing Right Now

- Your fiat dollars - backed by nothing except our government's word - have become worthless
- Your retirement portfolios of dollar-denominated stocks will soon be obliterated
- Your savings and pensions - already steeply in decline - will dwindle to nothing

Shockingly, the Fed has more than doubled the money supply in just the last two years. This means you have been legally robbed of 50% of your money! In a misguided attempt to triage the debt problem, they will continue to dilute value by flooding the money supply – until the mightiest currency on earth has become worthless paper. History will repeat itself all over again as the dollar goes the way of all historical currencies on its journey to oblivion.

However, There Is Some Good News...

There are two sides to this story. Because of the changing rules of money, the greatest transfer of wealth in the nation and the world is now unfolding. Money is about to flow away from the financially uninformed and flow towards the financially well-informed in the years ahead.

I am sure you are aware of the rising price of gold that's been going on for almost 10 years now. Most recently, gold started climbing with even greater speed. History repeats itself again and again. Whenever governments start to dilute their money investors transfer their money into gold. Gold has intrinsic value and will always prevail in any economy.

What most non-investors and investors – including yourself – probably you don't realize is that although gold is a great way to preserve your wealth, it's silver that could actually make you rich!

The price of gold has already risen dramatically, but silver is just beginning its climb.

Many financial experts predict that gold could at least double to $2,000 . . . $2,500 . . . and some say even $5,000! But experts also predict the price of silver could rise seven to eight times its current value before hitting its peak.

What You Will Learn From 'Building Wealth With Silver'

You will discover why the Federal Reserve was created and why you and I have been kept in the dark about its true purpose. You will find out why the U.S. dollar is quietly being destroyed without fanfare and the reason this process is being publicly denied and covered up. You will see why unemployment numbers, along with many other economic figures, are rigged, and how we're are being lied to about their true significance.

Why Silver Is The Best Investment Opportunity Right Now

Get the facts on silver production and consumption, and all the details behind silver's projected five- to eight-fold increase over the next several months.

Follow the easy step-by-step instructions how to buy and sell silver to turn a profit every time. Use the power of leverage to multiply your profit by the factor of four without increasing your risk substantially. Get a glimpse of the economic outlook over the next 10 years so you can make the most out of today's investment.

Beware, this financial crisis is far from over regardless of what you may be hearing or being sold by the media. The stage is quietly set behind the curtain and the dramatic crisis will shortly begin to play out. Rather than being a passive member of the audience, it is your duty now to take action yourself.

Why not use your money wisely, enjoy financial literacy, and start profiting from your own silver investment? Heck, if you're like me, you'll even have a lot of fun in the process. Order your copy today - available at Amazon or Barnes & Noble.

RESOURCES

"Free Bonus Content"

Resources

For additional 'Wealth Advisor' editions please check our website or go to amazon.com.

Get All 'Wealth Advisor' Editions
www.wealthbuildingcourse.com/wealth-advisor

At present we are offering a free membership to the Wealth Building Course. This membership is free as long the full course is in development. The current release date will we in 2012 and the course will be priced at $799.

Sign Up For Your Free Wealth Education Membership:
www.wealthbuildingcourse.com

If you have additional interest in preserving your wealth and invest in silver please check out the author's book: 'Building Wealth with Silver', which is available at amazon.

Building Wealth with Silver Book:
www.wealthbuildingcourse.com/silver-book

The author also developed a very sophisticated course around silver investment, which is available for purchase online. The 'Silver Fortune Formula' course reveals every detail for successful silver investing.

Silver Investment 101:
www.wealthbuildingcourse.com/silver

Resources

Thomas Herold, CEO – Co-founder Wealth Building Course

Thomas Herold is a successful entrepreneur and personal development coach. After a career with one of the largest electronic companies in the world, he realized that a regular job would never fully satisfy his need for connection on a deep level.

The only way to live his full potential was to start building his own business and find new ways to be in service to others.

For over 25 years he has helped many people – including himself – build their dream businesses. Toward that goal, he focuses on education – simplified and enhanced by modern technology. He is the author of three books with over 200,000 copies distributed worldwide.

Other than his passion for creating businesses, Thomas has spent over 20 years in the self-development field. Placing emphasis on the exploration of consciousness and building practical applications that allow people to express their purpose and passion in life, Thomas's work in this area has provided ample and happy proof that this approach works.

He believes that every person has at least one gift and that, when this gift is developed and nourished, it will serve as a fountainhead of personal happiness and help contribute to a better, more sustainable world.

For the past three years Thomas Herold has studied the monetary system and has experienced some profound insights on how money and wealth are related. He has recently committed to sharing this knowledge in a new venture – the Wealth Building Course, a website along with educational materials that designed to help people get started on their own money makeover and get a financial education in the process.

Thomas's ultimate vision for the Wealth Building Course is to empower people to adopt a wealthy mindset and to create abundance for themselves and others. His ability to explain complex information in simple terms makes him an outstanding teacher and coach.